I0407212

Building Better Relationships

Short Essays on Learning to Relate

JULIE ROBERTS MFT

Building Better Relationships: Short Essays on Learning to Relate
Printed in the United States of America
Copyright © 2011 Julie Roberts, MFT
All rights reserved.

For information:
www.truceworks.com

ISBN-13: 978-1466376816

This book is dedicated to my Mother Adeline
and my three wonderful children.

~ The way we communicate
with others and with ourselves
ultimately determines
the quality of our lives ~

—Anthony Robbins

Contents

Acknowledgements 9
Preface 10
Introduction 13
Premises of TruceWorks 21

Section 1: The Evolution and Impact of the Parent/Infant Interaction on the Formation of Identity 23-29

Why do babies relate? 23
Why do parents relate to their babies? 23
The combined relation-seeking behaviors of parent and infant produce their relationship 23
The characteristics of parent and infant bonding 24
The impact of relationship on the formation of self and other 24
How does the baby develop a sense of self? 25
What happens if a parent cannot hold his or her own emotional boundaries? 26
How does the baby regulate the parent? 26
Regulation of the stress response is an outcome of the parent and infant relationship 26
Relational experiences impact our later feelings toward others 27
How does our experience form our identity? 27
How does our early relational world impact our cognitive development? 28
How relationship helps the baby learn to regulate their emotions 29

Section 2: Short Essays on Relationships and Their Disruptions 30-51

Overview: A relational model of development 30
Putting relating back into relationships 33
What are relational needs? 35
A list of relational needs 37
What are relational styles and how do these develop? 38
Styles of relating—negotiating autonomy and dependency 39
Balancing the need for autonomy with the need for connection 41
Using our relationships to regulate our emotions 42
Why are differences so difficult? 44
Why do we connect and how do we learn to do it? 45
The mutuality of connection 46
Basic skills of connecting are learned early in life 47
Staying emotionally connected 49
Deepening emotional connection in relationships 50
Bridging differences in connecting emotionally and physically 51

Section 3: Short Essays on Obstacles to Connection and the Impact of Disconnection 54-63

What is projection? 54
The stress of relationship disruption 55
Dealing with anger in relationship 57
Deeper levels of relationships 58
What is shame and why do we experience it? 60
Regulating our emotions with our addictions 62
How to survive the wound of betrayal 63

Section 4: Short Essays on the Causes of Conflict in Relationship: A Relational Model 68-76

Difficulties in relationships: An overview 68
Conflict resolution—preventing conflicts from escalating 71
The anatomy of a conflict 73
What causes a relationship conflict to reach an impasse? 74
What happens when our emotional needs are not met? 75
The "I'm right and you're wrong" trap 76

Section 5: Short Essays on Conflict Resolution in Relationship 78-83

How to move through difficult times 78
How to end conflicts by listening 80
Conflict resolution: How to stop repetitive arguments 81
How to be present in your relationship 83

Section 6: Short Essays on the Importance of Communication in Resolving Conflicts 86-89

Five steps for effective communication in a relationship 86
How to improve communications 88
How incorporating feedback loops helps us communicate successfully 89

Section 7: Understanding and Using TruceWorks.com or the Mobile App 91-102

Intoduction 91

Origins and purpose of the CLEAR relational process 92

How the CLEAR process promotes connection 93

The CLEAR process is designed to facilitate a two-way feedback dynamic in a conversation 93

The CLEAR process is designed to mimic the early relational dynamic between a parent and child 94

How to use the CLEAR process on the website or on the TruceWorks app 94

The stages of the CLEAR process require answering the five-step questions and the two-step response form 95

From disconnection to connection 99

The five stages of the CLEAR process diagram 99

Who can use the CLEAR process? 100

How to use the CLEAR process on your computer 100

The TruceWorks Mobile App 102

Section 8: TruceWorks.com: Navigating the Website 103-107

How to get around the website 103

This section shows pages from the website and has a brief description of what happens when you use it

Acknowledgements

I would like to acknowledge my three friends: Joyce, Catherine and Arlene, who have been essential in the production of this small book of essays, the TruceWorks.com website and the TruceWorks mobile app. I am very grateful to my son David for having shared ideas with me in an ongoing and wonderful conversation over the years. I would also like to acknowledge the contribution of my clients for sharing their thoughts and feelings with me; I have learned so much from each of them.

The ideas contained in these pages are not original; They are an integration of many, many theorists and researchers who have contributed their original work to the ongoing efforts to understand the human mind.

Preface

The idea of using a written interactive process on the Internet to facilitate relationships grew out of working with couples and noticing common obstacles in how they were communicating. These obstinate patterns in relational styles seemed to burden their lives unnecessarily. I began to wonder if a process which encouraged each person to consider each other's point of view in a less confrontational way would help.

It is not the intention of TruceWorks.com to be a substitute for face-to-face relating or counseling. On the contrary, it is to improve relationship. I consider human contact as something that is too valuable and too profound to ever replace. The purpose of using the process is to provide the experience of a more relational model of communication that can, hopefully, create more connection between two people.

In order to provide an interaction in which two people could practice communicating in a more relational way, meaning that each of the parties could express themselves and know that they were being understood by the other, we developed the CLEAR relational process. The communication model emerged from the research and psychological theory that places focus onto the impact of the relational context of human development. The process mimics some of the optimal communication patterns of the parent and infant.

For those who benefit from using the process, it might become an ongoing way of improving communication; for others, it might serve as a one-time help to clarify an issue or provide an opportunity for self-expression that was needed. For others, simply reading about the process could be enough to gain insights to improve their own communication style.

It became apparent that the educational value of the website was perhaps its biggest contribution. TruceWorks.com has become a website devoted to both education and practice in relationships. This book is part of an endeavor to provide instructive information both for how to use the site and, equally as important, to get a quick overview on the significance that relationships have in our lives from before birth to the day we die. It is hoped that with this information, conflicts will be easier to understand.

This collection of short essays is organized so that the Table of Contents serves as an outline for this mini-course on relationship as well as organizing an approach to TruceWorks.com and the CLEAR process. It is divided into eight sections. The first six sections are on relationships and conflict and the last two include explanations for how to use the website.

Introduction

Relationships: Learning to Relate

Background

Everyone wants to have great relationships. We are social beings. We spend the greater part of our lives in relationship with others. We form primary relationships and maintain deep primary bonds with our partners and our children. We often have long-term relationships with friends or co-workers, and we stay significantly connected with our parents and our siblings. We relate to many, many people in different roles and circumstances and we experience many levels of connection.

We develop and are sustained by being and feeling connected to other people. In the long history of the human race, it is a recent development that individuals can survive living alone. For those who choose to live alone or find they are alone, it remains outside the norm and often is a major adjustment.

Learning through experience

We learn to relate through growing up in relationship and are subject to the experience of the relational styles we are born into. Our own relational styles are formed through this experience. We are very lucky if the sensitivity and responsiveness to our needs is adequate so that we learn how to communicate our own needs as we learn how to relate to the needs of others.

Parents need more support

Unfortunately, these early relational experiences are often an uneducated and somewhat haphazard experience. Most people rely on child-rearing practices handed down through generations or brief education from a current pediatric theory. There is limited education provided to parents or to children to help make this original relational experience optimal. We are forced to depend on tradition in learning how to care for our young, which does not help in handling the intense emotional experience that taking care of a baby involves.

Limited preparation

Although relationships are central and vital to our lives, we, in fact, have to wing it in regards to many aspects of relating. Almost every mother has experienced the excruciating sense of inadequacy when finding that she is alone with a crying baby and has had too little preparation.

Too many less-than-optimal outcomes

While there are many wonderful bonds that children form with their best friends and schoolmates, there are also systemic relational failures in schools as children bully others, form cliques and essentially reenact the less-than-optimal relationship skills they have learned at home. Later, as teenagers and young adults entering the relationship- and mate-seeking arena, they have to navigate instincts and social pressures, usually without having any understanding as to how to approach these monumental tasks.

Following mate selection, whether we are heterosexual or homosexual or other gendered, we have to relate on a daily basis. Negotiating our own needs in a relationship, particularly when there are differences, is a skill we have learned only through default, usually due to the less-than-optimal experiences we have had. So many couples are deeply troubled as they face problems in their relationships with little or no understanding about what might be going on and/or how to communicate with the other person to resolve issues.

Relational skills can improve our relationships

The good news is that we can learn more about relating at any stage in our lives. Once we gain even a minimal understanding of what is going on in relationships and begin practicing more conscious communication, our experience becomes self-perpetuating. It feels so much better to communicate in a more relational way, and we gain so much more of a sense of connection and well-being that we can usually overcome our attachment to our old, resistant patterns of communicating, even when they feel like home.

Obstacles in communication can be overcome

Learning to be more relational as adults can feel challenging for those who have developed strong defenses to protect themselves; however, it is much easier than we fear. Trying to communicate more about how you feel is a good first step. Practicing listening and trying to attune to the feelings of others is a good second step. This can be as simple as just reflecting back to them what you have understood them to say. Notice that the feeling of connection increases as you are able to understand how the other person is feeling and also when they are able to reflect back that they get what you are feeling.

Connections can deepen through communication

There is no substitute for the connection that can be experienced by looking at the other person while you are engaging with them. In addition, physical touch is the most direct way of feeling contact. The experience of physical contact is deepened when a person is open emotionally. Opening emotionally can be supported by learning to communicate feelings so that the other person can relate to how you feel.

Relating is fundamental

So much more is understood now about how the early relational behaviors of parents with their babies can positively impact future social capacities. Even though the research is with babies, people of all ages respond well to relational behaviors. Feeling a mutual connection with another person is enlivening at any age.

A Connected Relationship Requires Good Communication

Overview

Good communication in our relationships requires having a good sense of yourself so that you can express your feelings and needs in direct, non-threatening ways. It means that you are aware of and accepting of your own needs so that you are not solely focused on defending them. It also means that your need to get your own experience validated does not override your interest in understanding the other person's communication. Thirdly, it means you can experience and express your frustrations when your needs are not met so that you are not stuck in a defensive position, because being defensive often includes projecting your feelings onto the other person and making it even more difficult to relate to them. And, finally, it means that you can be open and curious about what your partner is feeling or needing and willing to try to grasp the complexity of their experience even when it is surprisingly different from your own.

Communicating in relationships is like juggling

Learning to communicate in relationships is a little like learning to juggle, because the essential ingredient is to be able to hold in mind and relate to more than one thing at a time, at least to the many layers of our own experience and hopefully to those of the other person. Watching the interchange of two jugglers as they toss and catch several objects between them comes close to what happens in a conversation when both people are aware of the four operations that need to happen in a related conversation. Both members need to be aware of sending their own message and its impact on the other, while simultaneously being able to receive the other's intended message and track its impact on us. Understanding that there are at least four operations that happen in a communication is not typically grasped.

Learning to be aware of our own needs as well as those of the other

This can be particularly difficult to learn because a big part of our psychological history is absorbed in developing a sense of ourselves and learning to express ourselves, both of which require that others relate to us. Because we have many needs in relation to others that involve their hearing and accepting our experience, we are typically busy trying to get our own needs met by others and then we have little room for relating to their needs. Sometimes people do not grasp that part of what they need to do in a relationship is to learn how the other person experiences things. We get so absorbed in our own experience and our own need to have our experience validated that we do not learn to relate to what is going on with the other person.

How we communicate reflects our early relational history

Some children have it easier than others. They have caretakers who are able to pay close attention to how they are feeling and what they need. These children have been taught how to express their needs and they feel secure that their needs will be met. They learn to regulate their own emotions in these early relationships where they have learned to negotiate their own needs with those of others. Because most of the time their needs are related to, at those times when they are not, they still feel the ongoing sense of responsiveness they are accustomed to. Growing up in an environment in which people are encouraged to say what they feel and think and connect to what they need makes it much easier to listen and take in what other people are feeling or needing. Later, as an adult, you can do this in your relationships.

Early life frustrations create later communication difficulties

For other children who do not have their relational needs met, sometimes simply because there is no awareness of these kinds of needs, the feelings of anger and hurt and disappointment that they incur, if this situation is chronic, become a problem in later relationships. Old feelings of frustration often get associated with and triggered by any relational situation that evokes similar feelings of not being responded to. If we are uncomfortable or unskilled at expressing anger, hurt and frustration, we run into further difficulty.

What are communication difficulties?

One psychological option we are left with is to act out these feelings in indirect ways, often withdrawing and cutting off the relationship. Another is resorting to self-destructive behaviors. Similarly, when we have not learned to regulate these emotions, we can become abusive, striking out either verbally or physically trying to express our frustrations, in the only way we feel we can.

What causes communication difficulties?

Sometimes these feelings have been put away because they seem too big to handle as children. In this case, as adults we find that we unconsciously project them onto the other person and see them through the eyes of our earlier experience, not as the person in present time.

Many people never question their perceptions of emotional events. They never realize that how they are experiencing something is highly original to them and is made up of the many associations they make to the behaviors or words of the other person. These associations to current experience are drawn from a lifetime of personal experience. We each interpret the meaning of events in a very unique way.

Because we always create a picture in our minds of what the other person has said or done, we use our pictures to develop our reaction— our narrative about what is happening. We create our own reactions; they are not caused by the other person. Our reactions contain our whole unique emotional history. They are like little emotional autobiographies. We think we are having clear perceptions of the other person, but in fact we are usually re-creating our own history.

We cannot relate to the other person by holding onto our own pictures

It is these pictures, or representations, of the other person that are the hardest obstacle. When we hold another person in our minds only with our own picture, we are not actually relating to them. We are actually relating only to ourselves because it is only our picture of them.

This picture can prevent us from seeing the other person or relating to their reality. Being able to open up a space in our minds to take in the other person's experience of something is a different thing altogether. At first this can feel disorienting. We have to suspend our own picture, particularly if it is a habitual one, and open ourselves to the possibility that we are not getting what the other person is experiencing.

The solution takes practice

Being able to hold the experience of the other person and your own reaction to it simultaneously requires being able to think—to be conscious while we are experiencing an interaction. It does not mean losing connection with your own feelings; it means being able to communicate your feelings and thoughts without blame so that the other person can take in and validate your experience.

When the other person takes you in, it is easier for you to reciprocate by being able to provide the same thing for them. Usually, when both people feel understood, a flow is created in the communication— the jugglers pick up the missed toss and continue.

What Is the Purpose of the TruceWorks Website?

The purpose of TruceWorks.com is to bring attention and understanding to the relational basis of our lives. Because relationships play such a big and obvious role in our lives, we are not always aware of the many layers of impact they have on us, i.e., how they facilitate our biological, social/emotional and cognitive development and our well-being throughout our lives. Only the tip of their significance is revealed through the wide range of reactions we have when we experience a disruption, whether lasting or simply temporary.

When disruption occurs without adequate inquiry and understanding of the development and significance of our relational lives, it is more difficult to understand our emotional reactions or to have the perspective or ability to prevent or repair disruptions.

By learning more about the broader and more subtle impact of relationship on us, we can understand why we have such strong needs to relate and we discover why disruptions are so emotionally difficult. Hopefully this inquiry will impact our current relationships by both supporting the formation of deeper connections and imparting the knowledge and skills to repair or prevent disconnections.

Most of us are not taught any fundamentals as to how to communicate in a relational way, nor are we taught how to repair the disruptions in our relationships. "Say you are sorry" has served as a coverall for the vast complexity of human interaction. Therefore, each person is forced to reinvent the wheel and struggle to deal with disruption with more or less success. Often feelings get left unspoken in the effort to reestablish a connection, only to come gushing back to fuel the next disconnect.

TruceWorks.com is designed to provide an educational and experiential boost to relationships by teaching through the materials available on the site and through the use of an online interactive relational process. The essays in the manual give a very rough sketch of human relatedness and its profound impact on experience. Using the process and learning through that experience helps develop the skills and information needed to better understand our own relational needs, i.e., how to relate more deeply to others and how to facilitate the repair of relational disruptions when they occur.

Premises of TruceWorks

We cannot overestimate the importance of relationship in child development and in our psychological world as adults.

Ruptures to our self-forming interactions can have a great emotional impact.

Conflicts reactivate our reactions to past disconnections.

Because we continue our need for relationship throughout life, when disruptions occur, they continue to affect us deeply.

Improving our abilities to repair relationships when they are disrupted is essential to our well-being.

More awareness, education and experience of how communication can build connection strengthens our relationships and prevents chronic disconnections.

Section 1: The Evolution and Impact of the Parent/Infant Interaction on the Formation of Identity

Early Relational Experiences Impact How We Learn to Relate

Why Do Babies Relate?

In the beginning of the infant's life, his or her drive to stay close to the source of warmth and nourishment produces not only their survival but a sense of connection. Both the feeling of safety and security that emerges by having needs met, including the concurrent experiences and expressions of pleasure, and conversely the experiences and signals of distress when these biological and emotional needs are not responded to, converge to produce the relation-seeking behaviors of the human infant.

Why Do Parents Relate to Their Babies?

The counterpart to the baby's behaviors are the caretakers' instinctive, biological and psychological desires to protect their young and to respond to the signals of the infant such as crying, smiling, agitation or relaxation. Parents have physiological reactions to the crying and agitation of the baby, which immediately focuses them on responding rapidly. There are hormones, e.g., oxytocin, that are produced by emotional reactions that support relational behaviors, such as nursing and physical touch, which in turn produce bonding.

The Combined Relation-Seeking Behaviors of Parent and Infant Produce Their Relationship

It is up to the evolutionary biologists to theorize how much the parent/infant interaction is determined by biology or by the impact of other environmental demands, such as having to keep the infant quiet to protect them from a predator or wanting to teach them how to protect themselves, or parents may simply be biologically programmed to be empathic. For our purposes, we are interested in the two sets of behaviors and the responses to these that draw both the parent and the baby into relationship.

The convergence of these two sets of reactions, i.e., the baby's and the caretaker's reaction to the relation-seeking behaviors of each other develops into the relationship. Even though there are many individual differences in the caretaker's and the baby's sensitivities to the challenges of the circumstances and events by which they are surrounded, nevertheless it is the means, i.e., the rhythms, the tempos of responses, and the emotional climate of this giving and receiving, that produces the overall nature of the relationship.

We see an individualized style of relating emerge from these back-and-forth signals, the meeting and matching of the signals of the other, and this creates a pattern and produces a unique bond. Within the matrix of this unique relationship, an individual human personality emerges.

The Characteristics of Parent and Infant Bonding

Classic attachment theory has identified four general types of bonding ranging from those that are more secure, less secure or insecure, to avoidant and, finally, what is called disorganized. These attachment categories generally describe the patterns created by the baby's response to the caretaker. More recently, theories of early relationship formation include looking at the impact on the mother's relation-seeking behaviors from the baby's response to her. For example, a mother can withdraw if her baby has timid or dull responses toward her.

The Impact of the Relationship on the Formation of Self and Other

Looking more closely at the subjective world of an infant, we see that the variations in their attachment category are associated with how they have learned to represent the other. Stored in the memories and associations in the baby's mind are their experiences in relation to their caretaker. These impressions begin to form into representations of their particular others.

Very generally, on the one hand, they form a representation of a sensitive other by the experiences of having their signals being sensitively attended to and matched contingently. On the other hand, if there has been a chronic lack of response and the infant has had to adapt to the absence of response, they form a representation of a non-responsive other. In between are the babies whose experience is so inconsistent that they cannot form a basic trust in the other. These are babies in the avoidant attachment category.

How Does the Baby Develop a Sense of Self?

If the parent can regulate his or her own feelings and can contain their baby's feelings, i.e., taking in and sensing what the baby is feeling and also remaining aware of one's own feelings, this helps the baby to experience a sense of their own separate self and begins to help form their ability to regulate their own feelings.

Going further inside the relationship between the parent and baby, we speculate on the formation of the baby's own subjectivity as a product of how they experience the subjectivity of the parent. We learn to relate to our own self (our subjectivity) by how we are related to. If the baby is closely related to by a parent and that parent can hold the baby's needs within her or his own personal boundaries, i.e., not become so merged with the baby's experience that there is little left of their own sense of having a separate self, the baby feels contained and develops a separate self. Through experiencing the flexible boundaries between self and other in the parent/infant relationship, a flexible and secure sense of self is developed.

What Happens If a Parent Cannot Hold Her or His Own Emotional Boundaries?

When a parent becomes overwhelmed by the baby's needs, there is often a tendency to lose connection with one's own needs and the experience of having a separate self. When this happens, a parent can become disconnected from the subjective world of the infant and simply projects their own reactive emotions onto the baby. The parent cannot include in their response a sense of the baby's needs because they are relating by reacting emotionally to the baby's needs.

How Does the Baby Regulate the Parent?

One aspect of the dialectic of the parent/child relationship that is often left out of the picture (because we are not used to looking at things dialectically) is how the baby's behaviors impact the behaviors of the parent. The baby is regulating the parent as well as the parent regulating the baby. A baby helps to reinforce a parent's feeling of successful parenting when they respond positively to the parent's attempts at satisfying their needs. If for some reason a parent is not able to feel successful because the baby is unresponsive or if for other reasons cannot relate, the baby's unresponsiveness can create disconnections which develop into negative feedback cycles between the baby and parent and difficult patterns emerge between them.

Regulation of the Stress Response Is an Outcome of the Parent and Infant Relationship

The vulnerability of the human infant and their parents to stress reactions and the well-known negative effect of having too much stress places the importance of the regulatory function of the relationship under further pressure. Being able to respond successfully to each other's signals most of the time seems to be a built-in imperative for optimal development. Most people have had the experience of a baby who is crying and is unable to be consoled. It is highly stressful.

Relational Experiences Impact Our Later Feelings toward Others

The experiences of how we are related to simultaneously create the styles or patterns of how we relate to others and to ourselves. When later in life we wonder why our partner suddenly seems exactly like our mother, etc., we realize we are unconsciously reexperiencing the same dynamic that we internalized in our early life with our current partner. Because these patterns form the templates for our relational experiences, we are bound to them to a certain degree.

How Does Our Experience Form Our Identity?

As we internalize our experience of an ongoing relational pattern, we form impressions and expectations of others that begin to form into a sense of ourselves in relation to others. These impressions, representations and expectations determine our everyday experience and start laying the foundations of our relational identity, how we see ourselves in relationship and how we see others. This is a basic part of the formation of our self-image.

We learn through our experience in two major ways. First, we add each additional perception from our senses to preexisting conceptions. We generate and store all the various associations that occur to us in our conscious experience. As we continue our awareness from moment to moment, our minds automatically access these stored associations/ memories (if they are not repressed) thus bringing our past associations to our current perceptions. How our minds organize this process determines how we experience things.

The other primary way we learn from experience is that we form identifications with it, in which we internalize whole chunks of experience. These chunks do not go through the same process of storage the way associations do, but are internalized as whole pieces of experience of our selves. These pieces build up as our identity.

We take in whole dynamics between ourselves and others—not only the behaviors, but the emotions, attitudes, proprioceptive attunements (how we feel the experience as something in our own bodies), the body movements and attitudes of others. Most of us have had the experience of suddenly sensing that we are acting exactly like someone else.

Because our sense of self grows and is both impacted by and impacts how we accumulate and internalize experience (either through the formation of associations or through identifications), we can localize much of our psychological development within the relational field. How we experience ourselves in relation to others determines much of how we form our own self-image. In turn, our own self-image impacts how we relate to others, so the dialectic continues and gets applied to other areas of our interaction with the world.

How Does Our Early Relational World Impact Our Cognitive Development?

It is just now becoming recognized in the world of developmental psychology how our early relational world impacts how we learn. It seems obvious that if we are open, receptive and secure in our relation to others that we would be open, receptive and secure in our abilities to imitate, listen, concentrate and in general digest new information.

A child who is defending him- or herself against reoccurring negative experiences or an absence of connection would seemingly be equally averse to taking in and being receptive to new information. A child who has to be hypervigilant to protect themselves may be focused more on surface signals of danger and not be as able to be open and receptive to a more complete digestion of new information.

Emotion Regulation: Internalization of Maternal Containment and Responsiveness

How Relationship Helps the Baby Learn to Regulate Their Emotions

Each time a parent soothes a child or pays attention to a bid for attention, the parent is providing the experience of external regulation of their child's internal state of mind. In this way, the child experiences the change from a fearful or some other distressed state of mind to a calmer or soothed one.

In like manner, when a desire for attention is met or negotiated with, the child experiences having an impact and gains a sense of their own agency. With this experience from the other, self-recognition is acquired and thus begins their ability for self-containment. The emotional reactions to needing something are regulated when the need is satisfied or negotiated with. The experience of responsiveness is internalized by the child. Through associative neural processes or identification or perhaps utilizing the mirroring faculties of the brain, he or she develops the mental and physiological function to do this for themselves.

Section 2: Short Essays on Relationships and Their Disruptions

Overview: A Relational Model of Development

The following short essay introduces most of the key ideas of a relational theory of development and so serves as an overview for the ideas that are developed in more detail in the articles that follow.

Beginning from our very early primary relationships and developing across time, we have a strong need to communicate, to express ourselves, to be understood and to understand others. We need the experience of someone hearing and responding to our signals. In this way, we learn that our basic needs will be understood and met, at least most of the time. We start to experience connection.

Learning to communicate is a challenge for both the parent and the infant. Ideally, through their experience with each other, both members of the parent/infant dyad learn how to relate: how to read each other's emotional states and physical signals. It is through this back and forth of relationship that our sense of self and other emerges and develops into the behavioral and emotional patterns that form our identity.

Infants learn by internalizing experience. An infant who has experienced timely and attuned responses learns to regulate his or her own emotions. By participating in reciprocal relationships, the infant also learns to recognize and relate to other people. It is through the experience of having our needs recognized, mirrored and met that a psychological self emerges. The quality of the attunement we receive from others helps us to form the mechanisms, both physiologically and mentally, to regulate our emotions.

Our attachment styles also reflect the nature of this attunement. A secure attachment reflects close attunement, whereas an insecure style reflects less attunement. These relational styles impact the way we relate throughout our lives.

It is important to the developing infant that his or her emotions register with the caretaker, so that these early feeling states are understood and responded to appropriately. The infant internalizes these experiences of a synchronized, or matching, "call and response," and this process reinforces the infant's innate sense of mutuality and connection to others.

Of course, no parent can always match the signals of a baby, but getting it right enough of the time is important, as Donald Winnicott's useful idea of the "good enough" parent proposes.

When the inevitable disconnections do occur, it is important that the parent and infant have learned how to reconnect, so that both members experience and trust that repairs to their sense of connection can be made relatively easily. Internalizing the experience of an easy boundary between separateness and connection helps to develop a secure sense of self.

When babies experience a constant mismatch between their signals and the responses they receive, a sense of disconnection is created. Chronic disconnection creates stress and negatively affects the baby's development. There are many individual variations in the baby's reaction to this lack of attunement. Some babies withdraw. Others make heroic attempts to adapt by relinquishing their own needs. These infants focus on attuning to their parents' needs and end up feeling disconnected from their own needs.

There are long-lasting consequences when these early relational needs are not attended to. Most of our styles of relating, e.g., outgoing, assertive, emotionally expressive or withheld, etc., and communicating, e.g., saying directly what we feel or often feeling misunderstood, are learned in our early experiences and set the templates that follow us throughout our relational lives. The same frustrations we suffered in not being responded to sensitively early on emerge over and over again. Present-day relational conflicts mirror these early relational failures.

Some of our basic needs such as hunger, comfort, warmth, contact, safety and being loved seem obvious. Other needs that form the basis for building attuned relationships are more difficult to see. For instance, our need for a response to correspond to what we need or are expecting is not necessarily obvious. This need for a contingent response means that when you are hungry, you expect to be fed, and when you are afraid, your need is to be comforted rather, not fed. Most of us continue to be frustrated by a lack of contingent responses. We often get upset when our intentions or meanings are misread.

Another important communication skill that carries over from childhood into our present-day relationships is the ability to join our attention with another and to attend to what the other person is focusing on and vice versa. Babies begin to look toward an object that another person is pointing at in the early months of life.

Following this development, they themselves begin pointing and expecting others to join them in their focus. The experience of joint or co-attention gives us further knowledge of other people's minds and our relationship to them. Being able to share our intentions and our meanings allows us to feel connected to others' thoughts and feelings, which is necessary for all learning and is particularly important in learning language and using words to communicate.

Over time, babies learn to express their basic needs in more symbolic forms. Evolving from crying, whining and other physical gestures to the shared meaning of sound symbols—i.e., words—is a major developmental task. We develop this capacity for shared meaning in relation to others who are reflecting back what they hear from us. We then hear and imitate their sounds. This reciprocal development not only gives us our beginning language skills, but also a growing sense of self as we get our meanings, our feelings and thoughts reflected or recognized by others.

The need to receive recognition in our relationships is ongoing. Recent evidence of the functions of mirror neurons, those capacities of the brain to experience the intentions of others and to sense another person's experience directly, adds another dimension to an understanding of our innate relatedness. Questions arise as to the impact on relationships of this ability to tune in so directly to other people and how this empathic connectedness interfaces with how we learn to relate to others. Lack of connection may be experienced as fundamentally against the human grain.

Putting Relating Back into Relationships

A key ingredient in relating consciously to others is to assume that the other person's behaviors, thoughts and feelings are meaningful. Then it becomes our task to learn what that meaning is. We may not immediately understand the meaning of certain behaviors, so it is critical that we replace our tendency to react, judge or dismiss with an interest and curiosity about what is going on. When our goal is to discover the other person's intent instead of drawing our own conclusions, a relational possibility opens up in the relationship.

We are not the only game in town

One of the main reasons that this is difficult is that when another person does something that causes us to react, we disconnect. We disconnect from them because what they are doing makes no sense to us. We may react to their behaviors by feeling hurt or angry.

When we view another person's behavior only through our own perspective, i.e., how it impacts us or how it makes us feel, we exclude the possibility of other meanings. We exclude them from occupying a relational space with us.

Finding ourselves caught in an emotional reaction to them, we have little interest in what is going on with them. Our reaction has now created a memorable scene about what they have done to us, how crazy their behavior is, etc. We then bring all of our own associations to these feelings.

Unfortunately, our reaction often has nothing to do with what the other person is trying to communicate. Our reaction creates a new and highly subjective interaction with ourselves that compounds an already difficult disconnection.

We are playing our own game by ourselves

The first and hardest part of changing these patterns is to realize that our minds create our reactions. We create both how we experience the other person and our reaction to them. For example, when someone expresses anger at me and I automatically get enraged, I now am seeing their anger through my own angry lens. My mind is forming mental and emotional associations to their anger and then judging or dismissing the person. I turn them into an alien object, the hurtful other. I am actually reacting to myself, my pictures and my stories. Usually we are not conscious of how our minds are creating our own experience of the other person's behavior. How we experience them usually has very little to do with them or their anger. This same type of interpersonal reaction can happen over and over again, so that we seldom if ever actually connect to the other person. It is very hard to keep our reactions separate from what the other person is experiencing.

Playing together has more meaning

Why does this matter so much? It matters if we are interested in establishing a real connection with the other person, one based on mutual understanding. Creating a real connection means discovering how the other person is constructing his or her experience.

It is one thing to understand yourself and see how you react to another. This can be a lifelong practice, slowly gaining the internal silence to actually look at your reactions as they arise. It is a totally different thing when you take in and understand what someone else is feeling and what meaning their behavior is having for them. Understanding another person is a very different event from understanding the impact they have had on you. Of course, in the process you may also need the other person to understand what impact their behavior has had on you.

Emotional contact creates a new game

Emotional contact with another person happens when we are being understood and received or at least an effort is being made to do that. Connecting to your own self is important and expressing yourself to another helps, but part of the equation for true connection and feeling emotional contact is the experience of someone else taking in what you have thought or felt. The experience of contact can happen both in being received by another person and in the act of receiving them.

It is sometimes enough that they have simply shown interest in how you have felt, even if they do not understand your whole experience. The critical thing is that they have been able to turn their attention to your experience and they have assumed that your experience has meaning apart from how they experience it.

Our Relational Needs Impact How We Relate

What Are Relational Needs?

Here is a more concise look at what relational needs are and what impact our relational needs have on relationship.

To a great extent, our identity is formed in relationship. Our psychological self develops and is sustained by the many experiences we have with others. Children grow up identifying with those around them, taking on specific characteristics and behaviors. However, it is through our relationships with others that our sense of self and our sense of other develop. Our self-identity is greatly impacted by how our needs are related to both in our early life and in our adult relationships.

Development and impact

As infants, we have many relational needs, starting with the biological needs for warmth, nourishment, protection and contact.

There are other relational needs that sustain the development of our sense of self that are sometimes less obvious. In particular, having our feelings and needs understood and reflected back to us through appropriate responses gives coherence to our sense of self.

It is through having our relational needs met that we learn to relate to others and form our self-identity. Our identities are to a large degree formed by the experience of having our needs related to or not. These experiences accumulate and become a part of our psychological structure.

If we feel we are loved and nourished, we internalize this into our experience of self. We internalize not only the feeling of being loved and nourished, but the capacity for loving and for nourishing others. These internalized experiences form emotional templates that will impact all of our relationships. The absence of having our needs met is likewise internalized and impacts our relationships.

Current relational needs

Because our relational selves continue to grow throughout our lifetime, we continue to need others to supply us with responses that meet our relational needs. Being aware of these needs is important because as adults we have to learn to manage our own needs.

As adults we find others who can meet some of our needs and we learn ways to handle our needs when they are not met. Becoming more aware of these less obvious relational needs makes it easier to understand ourselves and some of our complicated emotional reactions.

A List of Relational Needs

These are some relational needs that are met/not met in relationship.

Attention: Needing the other person to be focused on and attending to what you are saying or doing.

Understanding: Needing others to grasp the intended meaning of your words or actions.

Contingency: Needing others to respond to your actions or words in ways that you expect.

Joining: Needing to be able to share meanings and values with another person or group.

Recognition: Needing others to see and hear you and give value to what you are doing, being, thinking and feeling.

Respect: Wanting others to listen and respond to your feelings and needs with the sense that they value you and treat you as an individual with your own values and boundaries.

Security: Needing to feel that your environment is safe, that you are protected and do not have fear that your boundaries will be violated. Needing to feel that you matter to others and that you are cared for.

Dependability: Needing to feel that you can rely on others and be able to trust that they will act and speak truthfully.

Mutuality: Needing to feel a sense of balance with others that you both are giving and receiving equally.

Connection: Needing to feel on the same page with others. Needing to feel a part of a relationship or group.

Affiliation: Needing to have a sense of belonging. Needing to have friendships and feel part of a group of your peers.

Intimacy: Having a sense of closeness to special people you relate to. Feeling emotionally and physically connected.

Autonomy: Experiencing your own need for independence, wanting and able to do things on your own and in your own way. Having your own space in a relationship.

What Are Relational Styles and How Do These Develop?

In the beginning of our lives, our relational styles are configured by the accumulation of our experiences of being related to by caretakers/parents. We develop our sense of self in relation to the responses we receive to the signals we use to express our needs. These patterns of call and response form the type of attachment we make. There is a wide range of possible relational configurations, extending from feeling supported and securely attached to feeling anxious or disorganized.

Each person seems to have an inner relational landscape constructed by their own representations of connection, reconnection and disconnects. How we construct our representational terrain creates the spectrum of emotional and relational styles.

Because we need to feel our needs are appropriately responded to for a positive sense of self to develop, it is critical to be able to negotiate reconnection when we experience the inevitable disconnects. If, as children, we have too many disconnections and not as many intervening experiences of reconnection, any current disconnection is experienced as finality. These spaces, instead of being filled with the anticipation of good feelings of reconnection, are empty or panic-filled black holes, offering no return. We start to feel shame about our own needs.

We definitely cannot always get the response we need. It is the "good enough" baby/parent (a parent or baby that most of the time responds to what the other person needs) negotiating everyday life together that weaves the relational structures that support an ongoing sense of self and other—the patterns they develop and internalize that serve as a blueprint for the construction of all of our future relationships.

Styles of Relating—Negotiating Autonomy and Dependency

We negotiate our needs for autonomy and dependency. Our relational styles reflect the outcomes of these emotional negotiations.

We develop into adults through the early caring we receive from our parents or early caregivers. Simultaneously, we form attachments to those who meet our basic needs. There are many individual variations in the types and qualities of the attachments we form with our caretakers. Despite these variations, we depend completely on our early relationships to survive, both physically and psychologically.

It takes both time and maturity to develop a stable sense of having a separate self—feeling our independence from our attachment relationships. Our sense of having a separate/autonomous self is important to our psychological growth, but because we continue to need others to sustain our social/emotional needs, this need for independence can be experienced as an emotional conflict. Finding the balance between our need for independence and our dependency on others is an important psychological achievement.

Because there are many individual variations in the quality of our formative relationships, each individual finds their unique way of negotiating the tension between their need for independence and their dependency. These uniquely developed patterns of relating determine our relationship styles.

A person who has had a secure relationship in childhood may find it easier to deal with solving the paradox of these two opposing needs. They are comfortable with both feeling independent and their dependence on others. Whereas someone whose attachment is insecure might have a harder time feeling their own separateness, their experience of the lack of connection could cause them to feel dominated by their need for others. Such a person may seek constant approval from others. Another pattern is that of the person who fluctuates between the two needs, sometimes feeling strong needs for others and at other times having an aversion to closeness.

We each enter our relationships bearing our individual histories of attachment styles and also with our particular style of dealing with the tension between dependency and autonomy. These established psychological patterns determine our tolerance for emotional closeness as well as the amount of autonomy we require. For relationships to be successful, they must be able to adapt to each person's relational style.

If we are not aware of the existence of relational styles or of the tension between our dependency/autonomy needs, our relationships become battle zones where we fight for our needs. When we are unconscious of the underlying reason we are fighting, one person's need for greater independence may feel rejecting to the other person, whereas another person's dependencies may feel suffocating to the other person. By each person becoming more aware of their relational styles, the relationship can deal more consciously with their individual needs and negotiate successful relationship.

We need others to supply our relational needs. What happens when we have differences with the same people we need to support us?

Balancing the Need for Autonomy with the Need for Connection

How to "have your own space" and stay connected in a relationship

Feeling emotionally connected in relationships seems key to having a good life, although having this connection must not be at the expense of your own sense of autonomy. It is often difficult to find the balance each relationship needs between maintaining a sense of connection and providing each person with feeling free to have one's own separate space. If either partner loses their own autonomy, the relationship suffers.

It is often the case that in the beginning of relationships both members feel somewhat merged, being focused on the mutuality of each of their wants and needs. That is the honeymoon stage, when each person sees the other in an idealized way; the reality of negotiating their differences is in the background, for now, and there is not much distinction between one person and the other. Because the relationship is meeting some of the very basic needs for connection, particularly physically, there is little room for differences.

The next stage happens when differences come into focus. For instance, one person may need much more time to themselves than the other person does. Often this is problematic. One person can begin to feel that they are causing the other person to feel rejected, or the person wanting more time together can feel hurt and interpret their partner's need for alone time as rejecting and not caring.

Sometimes one or both members lose connection with their own needs, seeking connection only by trying to meet the other person's needs. Some of these behaviors are generous and empathic, but too much leaves a person feeling disconnected from themselves and consequently from the other person. A relationship in this situation has lost the balance it needs to maintain each person's need for connection and their own autonomy.

41

Having your own autonomy means being able to know and express what you need both from within the relationship and also what you need for your own separate self. This means pursuing your own interests, making connections with others outside of the primary relationship, when necessary, and having time for your own solitude.

Meeting your own autonomous needs gives you emotional energy and reserve to bring to your relationship. When each person brings energy to the relationship, it can grow and be more fulfilling.

Using Our Relationships to Regulate Our Emotions

This essay explains what happens if we cannot regulate our own emotions and we become overly dependent on our relationships to make us feel okay. It explains how we can learn to regulate ourselves if we have not learned how to do this. It also goes over how the relationship with the parent affects the development of emotion regulation.

The complexity of our emotional lives in relation to others is one reason it is hard to understand how we can help ourselves through our various feelings within and without our relationships. We need relationships in our lives for many reasons, but one of the less obvious uses of relationship is to help us regulate our emotional lives. Although relationships supply us with many of our deeper human needs for connection so that when they are disrupted we suffer, if we have not learned how to regulate our own emotions in our early relational experiences with our caretaking, we use our relationships to compensate for this lack of a regulating capacity.

Although our need for connection with others is vital to us in many ways, if we are unable to regulate, i.e., to think through our own feelings, calm ourselves down or sustain a feeling of aliveness, etc., we are at the mercy of our connections with others to do this for us. Unfortunately, this method makes us even more vulnerable, because if we are using our relationship for regulation, this puts extra pressure on them and makes them even more susceptible to ruptures.

In general, a relationship can provide us with a source of positive feelings about ourselves and in this way helps us manage our negative emotions. If our good feelings about ourselves are being largely determined by sustaining connections with other people, our egos become too fragile, i.e., if they are happy with us or us with them, we feel good about ourselves and our "others," or conversely, when they are angry with us we are angry with ourselves and/or we hate them. If we are overly dependent on others to make us feel okay, we are particularly vulnerable to even small disruptions in these relationships. Because we do not have the capacity to think through our own emotional reactions and contain them for ourselves, our emotions become volatile when those we depend on for regulating us are not available.

Using others to regulate our own sense of self is one of the contributing factors for becoming upset when there are disruptions in our connections with others. One aspect of our upset is that we are left with our own unregulated feelings and do not have the capacity to change them ourselves. We can get stuck in a negative state for long periods of time.

We learn to regulate our emotions in our formative relationships. A parent who soothes an upset baby, relating to the baby's emotional world over and over again, day after day, provides the baby with the physical and emotional experiences of having an upset feeling state transform into another "soothed" feeling state. These repeating attuned experiences develop, in the baby's mind, into mental/ emotional and neurological pathways, forming the self-regulating capacities.

When a caretaker is able to regulate their own emotions in the relationship with the baby so that they can make attuned responses to the baby's needs and feelings, the baby internalizes the parent's self-regulating capacities. The parent is able to contain the baby's feelings by translating their emotional experience into a mental experience, i.e., thinking out or sensing what is going on and figuring out what is needed.

When a parent is overwhelmed by a baby and can react only emotionally, they simply impose their own feelings onto the infant and are not able to sense the needs of the baby. This baby is left without developing enough of the internal mechanisms to regulate their own emotions.

While the capacity to regulate our emotions is hard to learn without having experienced it in an early primary relationship, it is very possible to achieve. We learn by doing for ourselves what a parent can do for a baby. The parent uses his or her thinking capacity to figure out what the baby needs and takes steps to meet the need. In the same way, we start to analyze what we are feeling, speculating on the causes of our reactions, imagining what it is we would need in the situation and how we imagine those needs to be met. We then try to get our needs met by expressing them to the appropriate people.

If we cannot get our needs met, like a related parent, we comfort ourselves by developing a strategy to deal with our feelings. We can simply have the emotions and accept that we feel disappointed, sad, angry, etc. By telling someone else how we feel, we help ourselves accept our feeling. We can develop an alternative plan as to how to get the need met by substituting some other need for the unmet one, or we can let go of the need and decide we can move on.

Why Are Differences So Difficult?

One of the reasons that differences or conflicts can cause so much reactivity is that when people disagree with us or are angry, we lose them as suppliers of our relational needs. We can learn to tolerate difference when we can temporarily suspend our relational needs, or we can supply that need for ourselves. A stable self can maintain its cohesiveness in the face of difference.

It is often difficult to hold onto a sense of connection when we do not receive what we need from others. We can feel negated when our needs or desires are not recognized. Our tendency is to immediately negate the other person.

Developing our interdependence and a sense of mutuality in our relationships helps to maintain a sense of connection that can survive the inevitable disruptions. A relationship that has developed its sense of mutuality supports each person in holding his or her separateness without disconnecting during a disruption.

It is hard to get a perspective on how much we need others to reflect our thoughts and feelings. Simply being aware of these needs and noticing our reactions when they are not met helps .In a mature relational experience we can feel connection with the other person and still be aware of our own separate boundaries, i.e., our own thoughts and feelings. Feeling disconnected means losing a sense of contact with the other person or with ourselves. As we develop skills in holding the tension between our separate self and our feelings of connection, we learn how to experience differences without disconnecting.

Why Do We Connect and How Do We Learn to Do It?

Connecting with others

Our feelings of connection with others sustain our sense of well-being. Understanding this vital element of our emotional lives can help us improve our interactions and deepen our sense of connection.

Often we have the experience of having a good connection with another person. Some of the qualities of this experience are intangible, hard to even begin to articulate and therefore are easily attributed to "chemistry" as a blanket explanation, whereas other qualities that contribute to having a good connection are more observable, in particular those elements in communication that contribute to feeling connected, such as a sense of mutuality or a sharing of experience.

Learning to connect with others

The development of the sense of mutuality has a long history, beginning in early infancy and growing across time as the parent responds to their infant's signals, giving them both a sense of shared experience and connection.

Recent research has shown that babies learn to recognize the intentions of others much earlier than we had thought, giving them many opportunities to develop their sense of mutuality. First they experience someone joining them in their world and later they experience joining with another.

The ability to join our attention with another, to attend to what someone else is focusing on and vice versa, also begins in one's early months. Babies begin to look toward an object that another person is pointing to. Following this development, the infant points and expects the other to join their attention with them. This experience of joint attention draws focus to the growth of the sense of mutuality, increasing understanding of other people's minds and our relationship to them. We learn how to connect to others so that we can participate in a shared experience.

The Mutuality of Connection

Our sense of connection in relationships depends on our sense of mutuality. The sharing of experiences builds a sense of mutuality so that the more of themselves each member of a relationship shares with the other, the deeper their sense of connection becomes.

All of us have probably had the experience of not speaking the same language as another person. By eliminating the basis for our shared communication, we find ourselves having difficulty relating. Our attention then becomes focused on the disconnection because we have lost commonality. Of course, there are ways to connect to other people that are nonverbal, but it is often more tenuous.

Likewise, if we are not sharing ourselves, we increase our focus on the disconnection. When we join our attention with another by either sharing actual experiences or through verbal expression, we bring focus back to the sense of mutuality and the feeling of connection. Expressing our feelings and needs in our relationship and being willing to take in and acknowledge the other person's feelings and needs creates mutuality.

How do we connect?

The ability to clearly express our feelings and needs and to hear and respond to those of others is an essential quality for maintaining a secure personal relationship. Our strong reactions to failures in receiving the responses we need in our relationships are a signal for how much we depend on our relationships to maintain an ongoing sense of well-being. Our reactions often bring up past experiences.

Basic Skills of Connecting Are Learned Early in Life

We often lack basic skills necessary to maintain our emotional connection in our relationships through communicating our feelings and needs and to repair disconnects when they occur. Our lack of skills can cause us painful feelings of isolation, affecting our overall sense of vitality and well-being.

We learn how to relate in our early relationships with our parents or caretakers. These early experiences create many of our capacities to form and sustain new relationships. Both parents and children learn from each other how to relate by learning to read each other's emotional and physical signals and states. Children learn to be aware of their own feelings by having their feelings recognized by their caretakers. We also learn how to repair disruptions when they occur.

Every infant needs to experience that the people in their environment hear and respond to their signals appropriately, e.g., their cries, movements and expressions. Some of our needs such as hunger, comfort, warmth, contact, safety and being loved are obvious; other emotional needs may be more obscure.

CONNECTION

One way we feel connection is by receiving a response that corresponds to what we need or are expecting. This need is not as obvious. Most of the time our signals will be understood and they will be responded to appropriately. This means that if you are hungry, you will be fed. On the other hand, if you are afraid, you will be comforted, not fed. In both cases, the responses match the need. Of course, no parent can always match the signals of a baby, but getting it right most of the time is important.

DISCONNECTION

If as children we have experienced a constant mismatch of our signals to the responses we received, we are left with difficult feelings of disconnection. Later in life we may have strong reactions when we are misunderstood.

A disruption to our sense of connection that can occur when we are misunderstood can trigger reactive states linked to early relationship disconnections. Without some developmental perspective, it is hard to understand why we often become so reactive. This is why a simple difference with someone can escalate into a complicated emotional situation.

RECONNECTION

Spending time focusing on what we need from our relationships, even very simple needs like wanting to be told if someone is going to be late, and expressing those needs can begin the process of bringing us back into emotional connection. Expressing our needs and getting them met leads to a feeling of emotional connection. Receiving and connecting to the feelings and needs of others also builds connection.

If we have lost touch with some of these fundamental relational needs, our lives can lack intimacy and we may experience an ongoing sense of alienation. Once we begin reconnecting to our own needs and expressing them, not only will we feel more alive, but we will often find it much easier to accept and respond to the other person's needs.

Staying Emotionally Connected

Staying emotionally connected to another person is one of the deepest and most basic needs that we have. Yet because we can still function well in everyday life when we are emotionally disconnected, we sometimes continue on, never realizing what we have lost.

Losing emotional connection with our significant others can happen gradually when we store up feelings without expressing them, or it can happen abruptly through the occurrence of one particularly upsetting event. If we do not repair the connection, a breach can turn into a continuing sense of alienation. We might find ourselves feeling depressed, not recognizing that it is the loss of emotional connection that is at the heart of our depression.

Having a good sense of ourselves grows from being responded to appropriately in our earliest relationships. We depended on these relationships to supply us with responses that strengthened our positive feelings about ourselves and to teach us how to handle our negative emotions.

We gained feelings of confidence, competence and emotional aliveness from having our capacities and our emotions related to by our caretakers. When our earliest desires were recognized and responded to, we developed and learned to sustain a good feeling about who we were. We came to feel connected to ourselves and to others. The need to be responded to and to feel a sense of connection to others continues throughout our lives.

Because our sense of self depends on recognition from others, we form strong emotional attachments to those who recognize us. It is in our early emotional relationships that we have learned how to relate to other people's needs, as well as our own, so that later in life we can form lasting bonds with others.

We learn that relationship is not a one-way street, that the foundation of an emotional relationship is the sense of mutuality it generates. All relationships are sustained by the sense of mutuality in which each person feels connected to the other through the experience of each person being able to express their needs and having them recognized and responded to.

Of course, there are ways to adapt to not having our emotional needs met, and some people can manage well without this sense of emotional connection. These people learn to take care of themselves and live productive and creative lives, often forming life-sustaining interests. However, living without the sense of emotional intimacy that occurs when relational needs are being met limits the sense of security, contact and well-being that emotional connection provides.

Deepening Emotional Connection in Relationships

The drive for connection with others is partially motivated by the need to connect more deeply with our own emotional selves. Often we have lost connection with our deeper emotions and we live in our heads, mentally processing our experience without feeling much more than frustration or toleration. One reason we become out of touch with our own deeper feelings is that we have lost awareness of our relational needs—all the highly specific needs that we have in relation to others. It is through expressing these needs and having them met that we reconnect to the deeper levels of our own emotional reality, which creates more of a sense of our aliveness.

Often our relational needs get reduced to our desire for sexual connection. Although sexual relations can be an invigorating experience for our bodies, they can also illicit a terrible emptiness when the relationship does not engage our sense of emotional intimacy. Emotional intimacy happens when we are aware of and can express our relational needs as well as our physical ones.

One reason music is so appealing is that it touches our emotional centers and enlivens the experience of our feelings in amazing ways. Sometimes we connect to our feelings about other people by listening to a song. In the same way, when we express what we need from others directly, we start to bring ourselves back into a sense of our need for connection, both with our own feelings and with the other person.

Often, because we are unaware of many of the more specific needs we have in relation to others, we do not know what is missing in our relationships. Focusing on questions such as what types of responses we are wanting from the other person, for instance, what we would really like for the other person to say or to do, or simply how much time do we want to spend together or apart can start a deepening of relational awareness and add to the sense of emotional connection.

Bridging Differences in Connecting Emotionally and Physically

Although having a sense of connection to others is a basic drive, if you ask people to describe their experience of feeling connected to another person, you will come up with a large range of responses. Feeling connected is a highly subjective experience and every person has his or her own version of this experience. When two people in a relationship have significant differences in how they experience connection, it is important for each person to recognize the difference and work to appreciate the other's needs.

One popular theory of differences in how we connect is the idea that men feel connection sexually and women need to feel connected emotionally before they can connect physically. While this may be true for many, there are also many women and men who fit into the other sex's assumed category. There are many women who have a hard time connecting emotionally and have a strong need for physical contact to experience any sense of connection.

There are many people who can have an intense sexual experience, but at the same time feel very little connection with the other person. Some of these people have never felt emotional closeness. Others can experience connection only through emotional contact and cannot feel connected through physical contact. Those who do not experience emotional connection find the experience of the physical contact as the closest experience they can have of being connected to another person. There are others who feel immediate emotional contact through touch.

Because there are huge variations in how emotions get responded to in each person's history, there is a broad range in our capacities to think about feelings and express them. Similarly, there is a broad range in our capacities to relate to the feelings of others.

Many people have grown up in situations in which their feelings were not responded to. When feelings are not related to it is harder to learn to process our emotional experience. Instead of learning to express feelings so that we can feel connected to others through communicating our emotions, we carry our experience in body memories. We hold the emotional tensions of our experience in our muscle memory. Because we cannot effectively process our emotions and articulate our feelings, we are more dependent on our bodies and physical expression as a vehicle for connection. If body memories are predominantly traumatic, even this physical connection can become difficult.

Because the way in which emotions are related to influences our relationship to our bodies, children who have had parents who can respond to their feelings have an easier time integrating their emotions with their physical needs. They do not experience splits between connecting emotionally or physically.

Becoming aware of ourselves and our individual needs in how we can experience connection is a good first step, particularly if we are in a relationship where the other person has different needs. Understanding the subtleties of how the other person can experience connection is equally important.

Expressing our needs and talking about our differences can build a new feeling of connection that can bridge an existing difference. It is much easier to relate to a person who has different needs if we have understood the complexity of their needs in more depth and have received their understanding of our needs.

Section 3: Short Essays on Obstacles to Connection and the Impact of Disconnection

Psychological Mechanisms Influence Disconnections

What Is Projection?

Projection is an unconscious psychological mechanism that allows us to block and disown certain aspects of ourselves—feelings, qualities—and to cast them outside onto others. We often project our own thoughts and feelings onto others instead of experiencing and being conscious of them. We imagine our feelings and thoughts belonging to the other person.

Becoming aware of our projections is necessary in order to have better communication with others. When we project our thoughts and feelings onto other people, we cannot relate to what they are actually saying or doing. An easy way to check out whether you are projecting is to ask the other person what they actually are feeling or thinking.

In infancy we use projection as a psychological defense against overwhelming emotional experiences. As we develop a sense of ourselves, we learn to differentiate our own feelings from those of others. Those feelings that are unacceptable to us, we project onto others.

For instance, if we are feeling angry with another person and we are uncomfortable with that feeling, we disown it and experience the other person as being angry with us. In that way, we don't have to experience our own difficult feelings.

In our early relationships, we experience ourselves in relation to the other important people in our world, collecting many different thoughts and feelings. Over time, we construct patterns of relating, associating specific sets of emotions, behaviors and expectations to each relationship.

When we enter into our adult relationships, we bring with us these preconstructed patterns. If in our current intimate relationships we find ourselves repeatedly falling into habitual reactive patterns, it is often the case that we are projecting these older patterns onto our present experience. Recognizing these repeated, familiar reactions can help us to move beyond our reactivity, often the cause of conflict.

The Stress of Relationship Disruption

The need for connection

Awareness of the depth of the need for connection with others is being made more and more apparent each day by the explosion of social networks. In the past, our needs for connection have been viewed as the by-products of instinctive and biological drives that have kept our species going.

Attachment theory is based primarily in the biological need for proximity. More recently, ego psychology and intersubjectivity have explained how the self grows in relationship, focusing more on psychological development than the needs of the body. Because of the emphasis on these needs for connection/relationship in human life, the other side of the coin, the impact of disconnection, is simultaneously brought into focus.

Disconnection—the other side of the coin

Relationship disruption comes in many forms, from the extreme disruption of death of a loved one through divorce, conflicts, broken or angry hearts to simply waiting for someone to call back. Our reactions are likewise as varied as these varying circumstances; there are individual differences in tolerance for loss.

Emotional reactions to relationship disruptions

There is a full range of emotional reactions. We grieve, we feel depressed, we feel isolated, we get angry, we withdraw, and sometimes we feel shame or guilt. We can become caught in obsessive thinking about the loss: What could we have done wrong, or was there something that would have changed the outcome? We can be filled with anger, resentment and blame for varying time periods. Some people hold onto negative feelings for years after a disruption.

Skills are needed for reconnecting

In some of these situations, the disconnection is permanent and grieving the loss is an important part of acceptance. However, in many of these situations, there is a desire and a possibility for reconnection, but often we are unskilled in this department. Unfortunately, if we have not had training through life experience to find an easy way to reaffirm the connection, we suffer even more. Both the loss of connection and the problems with reconnection have a physical as well as an emotional impact on us—stress.

Stress produced by relationship disruptions

There is the obvious stress of traumatic loss, but not so obvious is the stress of milder forms of disruption such as conflict or other forms of emotional or physical disconnection. In each of these situations, we suffer stress from being disconnected from a person whom we typically rely upon to meet our relational needs. It is this aspect of the disconnection that produces a stress response.

Learning to repair disruptions reduces stress

Even small babies have a stress response when they are confronted with a parent who does not respond to their needs. If the baby/parent can easily reconnect, the stress response does not occur. Hopefully, with more understanding of the early origins of the stress response, we can learn how to reduce the stress caused by relationship disruptions in later life.

Dealing with Anger in Relationship

Aggression seems to be a part of human nature. It certainly is a part of modern societies. If we lived in a world where we easily received everything that we needed or desired, perhaps we would not experience it as often. However, we live in a world where many people are aggressive because they are forced to struggle for daily survival, and it seems that even if we no longer struggle for material survival, a certain amount of aggression is needed to facilitate everyday living.

Unfortunately, most people's egos are capable of generating large amounts of aggression with very little provocation. If we have not learned how to regulate our aggressive tendencies in our early relationships, we become victims of our more reactive aggressive emotions, such as anger, and have difficulties in relationships both with others and with ourselves.

There are two common ways of handling the unregulated emotion of anger. The first is that we project it onto other people and experience others as feeling angry toward us, not realizing that it is our own anger that we are viewing as coming from the other person. The other way is that our aggression and anger is repressed and it is unconsciously turned against us. Turning anger against the self is one of the primary causes of depression and also of developing self-hating narratives that cause various forms of social anxiety.

It is in our early relationships that we learn to regulate our impulses, most particularly our aggressive ones. Some babies seem to be more aggressive than others even as they seek nourishment from their mothers early in life. Some psychologists theorize that the young child's mind generates aggressive fantasies as a normal part of the unconscious mental processes.

Having a relationship where aggressive impulses are related to and contained can help the development of self-regulation and helps the growing child channel aggression in creative directions.

If a parent helps their child recognize and express their anger in words or more social behaviors, the aggression becomes integrated. This does not mean that the anger response goes away; it means that by learning to regulate emotions, the child learns to contain their impulses so that they can be channeled in more productive ways. Feelings can be thought about and not acted out. The child no longer needs to project the anger outside into monsters in the dark or develop negative feelings toward themselves. They learn to say that they are angry and talk about what is happening that is causing it.

As adults, we are also better off when we do not have to project our anger onto others, turning them into objects or turning our anger against ourselves. We can communicate better and stay in connection with others when we can experience our anger directly and express it in words.

Becoming Aware of the Impact of the Unconscious on Our Relationships

Deeper Levels of Relationships

What are enactments?

People are drawn to each other for many reasons. Some social science research suggests that like our animal relatives, we are attracted to each other through smell. A more psychological attractor is how the potential partner helps us reenact our usually unconscious relational patterns.

One of the amazing things about falling in love is how we find new experiences of ourselves that get enlivened by the attraction. On the other hand, when we experience the end of the phase known as the honeymoon, we run into what is known as our baggage. Our baggage is the habitual emotional reactions and expectations that we bring into the relationship.

How do early relationships impact current ones?

Our relationships are partly structured, for each person, by how well the other person fits into the roles and scripts of our unconscious relational expectations, both positive and negative ones. One of the hardest things to understand when we are immersed in relationships is the impact of what we are bringing to the current experience. Seldom are we doing anything new, although we do not realize this. We are behaving, mostly, in the same ways that we learned in our early interactions. Becoming aware of not being aware can be a first step.

How do relational patterns form?

Just as the use of our muscles develops our strengths, our daily and continual use of our relational capacities develops into relational patterns. Because experience is our teacher and because we internalize our experience into memories and associative patterns, we have already formed a template for our current relationships, long before we enter them.

Unconscious influences on relationships

It is profoundly difficult to realize the influence of the unconscious. Our egos are so busy trying to survive in our current relationships with ourselves, within our intimate relationships and with all of our social connections, that the idea that we are not aware of everything that is determining our thoughts and feelings never occurs to us. This understandable lack of perspective allows us only small glimpses into the impact of the unconscious patterns on our relationships.

Becoming aware of the unconscious

When we become curious about what might be going on in our relationships that we are not totally aware of, it becomes easier to recognize that many of our behaviors are simply reenactments or habits of earlier times. Sometimes a clue will come in saying something that you realize is similar to the voice or words of your mother or father, or you may sense a familiar bodily gesture of a parent or caretaker, or another insight may come from a character in one of your dreams that embodies ways that you feel in a real-life relationship. Accumulating these bits of evidence that support awareness of the influence of the unconscious begins the process of revealing how these patterns impact us.

Conflicts clue us into the unconscious

When we have conflicts in our current relationships, it is almost a sure sign that something is going on that we are not completely conscious of. Conflict can be used as an opportunity to explore and reveal how we are enacting old relational patterns.

A Relational Explanation of Social Anxiety

What Is Shame and Why Do We Experience It?

Introduction

The experience of shame, or of being acutely self-conscious, can be a very uncomfortable event, so much so that it often inhibits our activities, causing us to avoid circumstances that evoke it. There is a wide range of this type of experience, from simply feeling embarrassed that you may have said something you think was stupid to having a fully fledged panic attack when having to perform. Most of us are familiar with some form of social anxiety. Having some way of thinking about what is going on inside our minds during this type of experience can help us to relieve the symptoms.

What triggers shame?

Most of social anxiety can be thought of as a reaction to a break in a positive connection with others. Instead of feeling others as supportive and accepting, we imagine we are being exposed to evaluations or judgments. The feeling of being cut off from positive support right at the time when it is needed the most, and being subjected to critical judgment, real or imagined, produces the various iterations of a shame response. It is important to realize that the "other" can also be oneself, for at these critical moments we can be cut off from any possibility of self-affirmation, as well as affirmation from others.

What is a shame response?

Chronic disregard or misinterpretation of social/emotional needs produces shame in children and adults. Some of the physiological reactions to a shame experience are reddening of the face and neck area, heart rate increase, rapid breathing, trembling, withdrawal, and dissociative mental states.

These symptoms evoke difficult emotional experiences. Most people build up big defensive walls to protect them from feeling this way. Because it is hard to control the physical reactions, a person can also be ashamed of having the symptoms; this further perpetuates the anxiety. The symptom of disassociating makes it is harder to use our own thought process to help us out when we are reacting. When the mind has dissociated, our rational processes are not as available.

How does shame impact us?

In a regular state of mind, we record our experiences through taking in what we are aware of and forming a narrative about what has happened. This narrative is usually like taking notes on the experience—a more or less neutral record. If something uncomfortable happens, we can think of something to say, then remove ourselves and decide that it might be wiser not to engage in that situation in the future. We can make a rational decision about what has happened and direct ourselves as to how to think about it.

One of the complications of shame or of being overly self-conscious is that awareness has to be split into many parts. The usual rational thought processes are interrupted. We are now experiencing on several different levels of awareness, i.e., your perceptions, how you imagine you are being evaluated and how your body is reacting. Further, because we can be disassociated, we cannot create a narration to help guide us through the experience.

Regulating Our Emotions with Our Addictions

If our emotions regulate us instead of our regulating our own emotions, we are subject to using substances or people as a method to regulate ourselves. Because our feelings can be such a powerful force, we form powerful attachments to alternative methods of regulating our feelings. We can easily enter into an addictive relationship with a substance or person. Instead of having an internal mechanism that can make rational decisions to help us guide our feeling states, we become attached to an outside source to change and determine how we feel.

It seems to be the case that both not enough parenting and too much parenting can influence the development of addictive behaviors later in life. It seems obvious that if a child has not had enough experience in a relationship with a parent who has helped them to regulate their feelings by attuning to what the child needs that they would be lacking in self-regulating capacity.

Not so obvious is the lack of self-regulating capacity caused by a parent who has imposed too much regulation on the child by deciding for them what they need. This child has little experience in having their needs related to. It is through the experience of having our real needs related to and negotiated with that we internalize and develop our self-regulating capacities.

Without experience teaching us, it is hard to see that we can influence our own states of mind, i.e., we can learn to think about what is happening and take actions that change the way we feel. Usually, if we are in a negative state of mind, the physical and emotional state seems to control us. We need to learn that we can control it, to a large extent, by figuring out what has caused it and what actions we can take that can give us a different experience. Often overlooked is the simple experience of telling someone else how we are feeling or the fact that our bodies are feeling depressed because we are not using them.

Of course, there are circumstances where feelings have become too big for us to handle and we need the help of a professional or a group to form a more active and positive relation to ourselves.

How to Survive the Wound of Betrayal
THE PROBLEM

I think that every person has experienced betrayal in some form. For some people it can be very devastating. Although the reactions we have to betrayal are complicated, when we deconstruct them we find that they reflect many feelings and aspects of ourselves that we are usually not aware of.

Fortunately, when we become more aware of how our own, often unconscious feelings about ourselves are feeding into our reactions, our reactions can change. It is then possible to make clearer decisions about how to take care of ourselves in what can be a traumatic emotional event.

BACKGROUND

In childhood, as our sense of self develops, we need positive reflection and recognition of our thoughts and feelings to form and sustain a solid and continuous experience of ourselves in relation to others. When we are related to adequately the outcome is a positive self-image. We have the general feeling of being capable, lovable and acceptable. We can enjoy being with others in an alive and spontaneous way without feeling burdened by feeling compelled to please others to gain their approval.

When our growing self does not get recognized by having our relational needs responded to enough of the time, we learn to put away those needs. We are then left with the absence of the responses we needed and a feeling of being abandoned by others.

Most infants and children protest strenuously when their needs are not being responded to, and if this situation is chronic they have to adapt by abandoning their own needs and their protestations. As a child adapts, his or her negative feelings, i.e., protests, feelings of helplessness and hurt, are put out of consciousness. Each child in a situation like this develops new ways of relating to him- or herself and to others to compensate for the lack of responsiveness and to defend against further hurt.

WE LEARN TO COPE AT GREAT COST TO OURSELVES

There are many different coping strategies that a child develops when he/she is not responded to. One common way is to abandon our spontaneity and to dislike those parts of our own selves that do not seem to be acceptable. We conclude that parts of ourselves are not acceptable because no one is relating to them. In this way our more alive, spontaneous and expressive selves get put away into our unconscious minds. We adapt to unresponsive emotional circumstances by abandoning ourselves. Unfortunately, when we abandon ourselves it causes a great amount of pain and we are left with a fundamental sense of betrayal.

WE DEVELOP DEFENSES TO PROTECT OURSELVES

We survive by developing defenses that involve new ways of relating. These defenses protect us from feeling the pain of not having our needs met and having had to split off parts of ourselves. One way to protect ourselves is to try to become perfect in order to gain approval. In our attempts to attain approval, we form high expectations for ourselves and we become very exacting of both ourselves and others.

Another way we defend ourselves is to create rules that keep us safe. These rules determine the parts of ourselves (our thoughts, feelings and behaviors) that are allowed to exist and those that are not. As the rule keeper starts to predominate in our daily experience, we become highly self-conscious because we are constantly evaluating ourselves to see if we are following the rules exactly. We turn into judges and taskmasters, not only keeping ourselves on the "right track," but often being very judgmental of others, thinking that everyone should comply with similar rules.

HOW WE REACT TO OTHERS

When someone else behaves in ways that do not comply with our rules, we become outraged. We are outraged because the other person is allowing themselves to have feelings and obtain things that we are not allowed to have. We often narrate to ourselves the story of what they have done and how wrong they are over and over again, reinforcing the rules that we protect ourselves with, but at the same time reopening the painful wound of our own abandoned self. Because these narrations hurt us, they generate more and more anger.

HOW OUR COPING MECHANISMS INFLUENCE OUR RELATIONSHIP CHOICES

Our attractions to others are generated in large part by our unconscious minds. We often find ourselves with partners whom we later discover, sometimes painfully, to be quite different from how we see ourselves. Uncannily, it turns out that these same characteristics are very similar to aspects of ourselves that we have abandoned. We are often unconsciously attracted to those aspects of our partners that we do not allow to exist in ourselves. The relationship keeps us connected to those parts of ourselves, although vicariously.

CURRENT BETRAYAL STIMULATES OLD WOUNDS

When we feel betrayed by a person who is serving an unconscious purpose, we feel a traumatic sense of loss. Our loss is compounded because as we experience the potential loss of our relationship, we are simultaneously being re-exposed to the original loss of ourselves. We re-experience the wounding that forced us to put ourselves away in the first place. Our original sense of betrayal is re-experienced.

WHEN OUR RULE KEEPER IS THREATENED, WE ARE SHAKEN AT OUR CORE

At this point, we often focus on our outrage: how this person is breaking all the "rules." We are deeply threatened because these are the rules that have held us together. When our rules are challenged directly, we are exposed to layers and layers of feelings of abandonment that have accumulated inside us. This is an experience that can shake us at our foundation. For some people, one experience of this kind can keep them from forming intimacy for the rest of their lives. Closing down, shutting out and holding onto the rules with even more intensity is a typical outcome of feeling deeply betrayed.

HOW GAINING A PSYCHOLOGICAL PERSPECTIVE CAN HELP

Trying to put the current wounding of a betrayal within a psychological context helps us to understand the depth of our feelings. We can gain connection to our unconscious or disowned self through allowing ourselves to experience the feelings of the current loss. No matter how painful this may feel, we are simultaneously connecting to our disowned feelings. In this way, we can resurrect those aspects of ourselves that we have had to put away.

We abandoned ourselves because the survival of our psychological self was being threatened. We were not getting enough of what we needed from our environment to grow. We put parts of ourselves away to survive. We developed defenses to protect ourselves. Later we unconsciously picked our relationships to help us stay connected with our deeper selves. When our relationships are threatened, it feels as if our survival is threatened again.

A KEY REALIZATION

We can learn to distinguish the past from the present. As we connect to our disowned feelings, we reconnect to ourselves in a new way. We realize that we have survived the original threat. We have survived before and we will again.

During the original wound we were not able to think about what was happening; our only defense was to stop feeling the pain by unconsciously putting it out of our minds. We are now capable of experiencing the feelings and staying conscious by thinking about what is happening to us.

We do not have to stop feeling when we think about what we are feeling. By thinking we can understand our current experience. We can use our minds to guide us through the difficult experience of betrayal. We can change our experience from a traumatic replay of our history to a reawakening of a lost part of ourselves.

Section 4: Short Essays on the Causes of Conflict in Relationship: A Relational Model

Difficulties in Relationships: An Overview

Although the word "relationship" implies the existence of two minds with separate experiences, most people seem to have difficulties in relating to others as truly separate persons. This is particularly true when we are in conflicts.

We often identify too strongly with our own experience and don't recognize the other person at all, seeing him or her only as the cause of our reaction. We seem to expect that the other person's perceptions of an experience will be the same as ours rather than unique to how that individual actually experiences things.

Instead of being curious and attempting to understand the other person's point of view, especially if it is different from our own, we respond primarily by defending our own position, as if the mere existence of a different point of view is automatically a threat to our own. Often we assume that this difference makes one right and the other wrong.

In working with couples, one of the most frequent responses I hear when there are differences in describing an event or a conversation is, "That's not what happened." The speaker presents what she has perceived as objective truth and views any other way of looking at the experience not only as incorrect but often as proof that the other person is confused or crazy. Because each person's viewpoint seems to be negated by the other's, a defensive stance is automatically taken by both people.

The inevitable differences between any two people's minds, particularly the mental processes that are involved with how we experience events, conversations, other people's intentions, etc., are not often assumed or acknowledged by the couple. It would seem obvious that how we mentally organize our experiences—perceive events, associate to them, recall past events, etc.—is different for each person, yet this obvious fact of our differences sometimes becomes some kind of obstacle to how we experience others.

Differences can create a separateness that seems implicitly threatening. Each person seems to have a strong desire for sameness, for unity, with the other. Paradoxically, we require otherness to have our own experience validated.

Our resistance to perceiving others' experience as innately different from our own may be partly because of our persistent need to have our own experience mirrored, or validated, by the other. It is sometimes difficult to be conscious of our ongoing need for mirroring, our need for recognition from others. Yet, in fact, our earliest desires are often for our needs to be recognized. When we are not aware of this need for our experience to be recognized and validated by others, we sometimes make psychological demands on them in our attempts to get these needs met, often relating to them only as objects we use for this purpose. In our persistent quest to be validated, we can invalidate the other person's need.

Recent brain research shows how human minds have an innate ability to mirror another person's experience. Our minds can actually experience the other person's physical and perhaps emotional experience directly. When our own needs for being mirrored are unmet, we are driven to override our natural ability to mirror others, and we turn to defensive strategies to overcome this frustration— again at the expense of recognizing the other.

One common defensive maneuver used unconsciously to handle the frustration of not being able to get our needs met is projection. Our anger at the other person for failing us is projected onto the other person so that we see them as treating us in negative, angry, ways. We interpret the other person's behavior as having hostile or self-involved intent. For the person on the receiving end, this projection, which has nothing to do with how he or she is thinking or feeling, is often the trigger for feeling misunderstood and unrecognized. This cycle escalates the sense of disconnection between the two people.

Often we project our angry feelings outside of us and contain them in the other person so that we can prevent some of that anger from attacking us inside ourselves. Instead, we attack the other person with our angry judgments and our fears. The outcome of this defensive strategy is alienation.

On the other hand, being locked up in our own minds with persistently angry feelings that attack us through negative self-judgments and self-effacing messages is not an easy fate either. We can become isolated and sometimes masochistically bound to this angry part of ourselves. It is often a struggle to allow good feelings about ourselves to regain supremacy, as we are no longer able to experience positive feelings toward ourselves in the form of input from others. We get caught in a delusional negative feedback system. We use feelings of omnipotence or grandiosity to pump up our fragile self. We cannot experience the actual sustenance that comes through connection with others.

In order to experience a connection with another person, we need to recognize our projections, contain our own need for recognition by using our own self-awareness, and communicate our needs and feelings when the other person has the ability to receive them. We also need to be able to reciprocate by receiving and validating the other person's feelings and needs. When we express our own feelings and needs and have the experience of those feelings and needs being understood by the other person, we achieve a sense of connection with that person. We are able to ask the person for what we need as well as to relate to his or her own needs. In this way, our separateness becomes a means of feeling connection.

Conflict Resolution—Preventing Conflicts from Escalating

Whether we like it or not, to be human is to have conflict. We find ourselves disagreeing with the views of others. Sometimes what we want is in conflict with what others want. Conflict is one of the most universal experiences we as humans have and one of the most difficult. Being able to identify the common dynamics existing within conflicts can be helpful in preventing the conflicts we have from escalating.

When we are in conflict with someone, we have unmet needs with that person. In addition to the unmet needs we have with the other person, we often have inner conflicts with our own needs. It is usually easier to identify the needs we have with the other person than it is to recognize the inner conflicts we have with our own needs. Lack of inner recognition makes it harder for us to ask for what we need from the other person. Our inability to ask for what we need in a relationship may result in an escalating conflict.

Example

Let's look at a fairly typical conflict and see how interpersonal and intrapersonal dynamics escalate the conflict.

John has taken the family car to a mechanic for repair. His wife, Mary, needs the car to get to an important meeting and questions the delay in getting the car back. Mary complains that the delay will make her late for a meeting and she questions John's choice of mechanic. She reminds John that the last time they used this mechanic he seemed incompetent. She recommends trying a different one.

John reacts angrily to her challenge and recommendation and dismisses her upset about being late to her meeting as ridiculous. He declares that what is really important is being able to get the car fixed properly. Mary feels unheard, unsupported, dismissed and angry. The conflict escalates. Mary is angry because her interpersonal need to have her experience recognized and respected is dismissed.

It is harder to identify John's unmet interpersonal need because he has an inner conflict with his needs. As a child, he had very little of his experience mirrored or related to. Consequently, he has developed a vicious inner critic that constantly attacks him when he has any need. When a child's needs are consistently unmet, this is often the outcome.

John shoulders responsibility for decisions with great trepidation and anxiety. Even though he has some level of knowledge about auto mechanics, he is automatically vulnerable to "self-attack" when making a decision. The possibility that he will be punished internally if he makes a wrong decision places him under self-inflicted pressure. When Mary questions his ability to make a good choice, it triggers a cascade of negative self-judgments. These "self-attacks" are then projected onto Mary, whom he then experiences as the attacker. The conflict escalates further.

John is not able to express his need for understanding and recognition. He experiences a deep inner conflict in making a decision. John cannot express his needs to Mary and she is unaware of John's inner world. Mary has no idea that questioning his decision has caused him so much inner turmoil. At this point, the conflict escalates to an impasse.

Summary

This example points out the complexity of our reactions. The more aware we become of the dynamics that drive our conflicts, the more able we will be to prevent their escalation.

The Anatomy of a Conflict

How to resolve a conflict

To resolve a conflict, it is critical to learn to identify a few of the basic elements that form the anatomy of our typical conflict. Once we are aware of this basic anatomy, we can stop the conflict from escalating. Without this understanding, an everyday conversation can quickly turn into a situation that neither person can explain and that leaves each person feeling angry, helpless and disconnected.

There are two dynamics that exist in the basic anatomy of most conflicts. The first dynamic is interpersonal because it involves needs that exist in relation to another person. The second dynamic is intrapersonal, meaning we are having a conflict within ourselves; we have a need that we cannot accept in ourselves and, in fact, if we look closely, we find that we are attacking ourselves for having the need.

It is difficult to be aware of basic interpersonal needs and the intrapersonal conflicts we may have with them unless we have spent the time and energy needed to identify them. When these needs are unmet, as they are in a conflict, and we do not understand what is happening, our only option is to get hurt or angry.

An example of an interpersonal need is the need to be recognized. In our earliest experiences as infants and as young children, we have needed our experience to be recognized. If a child has grown accustomed to a world where what they are feeling and thinking is not understood and reflected back to them, they have great difficulties in maintaining a healthy sense of their own worth. They constantly need others to affirm them.

As adults, these children are still very hungry for the other person's recognition and acceptance. When this need is unmet it may instantly trigger many of the old and painful feelings we acquired in childhood.

However, our strong need for the other person to recognize our feelings without judgment is often interlinked with our own attitude toward this need. We may have an intrapersonal conflict with regard to this need, meaning that if we are not aware of it because we have had to put it away in our unconscious or we do not accept it, we will become even more reactive when our need is unmet by someone else.

If we have too little understanding of these aspects of the anatomy of a conflict, we become reactive and our conflicts escalate.

What Causes a Relationship Conflict to Reach an Impasse?

Often conflicts reach a stage where neither person in a relationship can see a way forward. Each may feel at the end of his or her rope, like giving up or ending the relationship. Thinking about ending a relationship is sometimes unconsciously used as a way to manage the difficult feelings that have arisen.

Feelings of helplessness and deficiency may occur when we cannot understand what is happening in our relationship. These feelings often get covered up by anger and self-defensiveness. An impasse is arrived at when we have become locked into a position where all we can do is defend ourselves.

One type of impasse arises when one or the other or both people in a relationship have emotional needs that are not being met. In most cases, this happens because their emotional needs are not being expressed. Sometimes we are afraid to express the needs that make us uncomfortable. Sometimes we do not express our needs because we are unaware of them.

When we are not conscious of our needs and our needs are unmet, we automatically get angry, sad, hopeless, confused—often not knowing why we are having these difficult emotions. It is easier to understand our feelings if we are able to connect them to our unmet needs.

When we are unaware of our needs, or we are not expressing them, we cannot contain or regulate our emotional reactions. The process of thinking through what we are feeling and expressing ourselves helps us to contain and regulate our emotions.

When we do not regulate, we become anxious. We may feel out of control. Then the only way we may know to regulate ourselves is to act out. We may express our anger in ways that the other person cannot take in. We may blame the other person or threaten to leave them. This escalation can push the relationship into an impasse.

When unmet needs accumulate they put pressure on relationships. Unmet needs often turn into resentments. Unexpressed resentments can push a relationship to a breaking point. When the relationship is at the breaking point, feelings that have not been expressed may come pouring out, releasing such a cascade of feelings that the relationship is pushed beyond what it can handle. The relationship has arrived at an impasse.

Another outcome of being unaware of our needs or not expressing them is that we do not try to get our needs met. We begin to lose touch with ourselves. We disregard our own emotional life. When we do not take emotional care of ourselves, we may begin to push ourselves beyond our own emotional limits.

What Happens When Our Emotional Needs Are Not Met?

We cannot feel emotionally alive when we are disconnected from our own needs. We are trying to run on an empty tank. This puts us in an empty and vulnerable state and we may place too much demand on our relationship to make us feel alive. It is often at this point that we look outside of the relationship to another person in an effort to supply our need for aliveness. Bringing in a third person easily develops into an impasse.

Instead of feeling good about our needs, expressing our needs to our partner and exploring which needs can be met in the relationship and which ones must be met in a different way, we start believing that unless we get what we need from the other person, we will not be all right. We put ourselves and the relationship under tremendous pressure that can easily push a relationship conflict into a lasting impasse.

The "I'm Right and You're Wrong" Trap

Discord

Often we get caught up in the content of a conflict. We establish that the other person has done something that has injured us, e.g., disregarded our rights, disagreed with our views, dismissed our feelings, etc. We fixate on the issue and decide that we are right and the other person is wrong. We aim, generally, to negate the other person and to inflate ourselves.

Why do we need to be right so much?

One reason that is often overlooked is that in a conflict we are cut off from connection with the other person—our relationship has been disrupted. If we are unaware of how much we need other people to supply our relational needs, we have no explanation as to why we get so distressed when they are disrupted.

Because we are at a loss when our relationships are disrupted, we have strong emotional reactions and we try to defend ourselves from some of the feelings triggered. One typical way we defend ourselves is to assume an emotional posture that relieves this anxiety, so we inflate ourselves with our rightness as a way of holding ourselves together. In this way, we do not have to experience the loss of connection and all the ways that relationship supplies us with our sense of well-being and aliveness.

Concord

The need to feel connection to others is at the core of our social existence. We are relational beings, from the beginning of our lives to the end. Babies grow, thrive and develop their sense of self in relationship. When we grieve the loss of a loved one, or a relationship ends, we get in touch with how deeply connected we are to others. We immediately experience how much we thrive in the mutuality of relationship and how much we can suffer from the loss of relationship.

Focusing more on understanding the nature of the loss we experience when we are in conflict can help us to regulate our emotional reactions. Connecting to our own emotions and expressing our real feelings can help us to move out of the right/wrong entrapment and it enables us to find alternative ways of taking care of ourselves. It is much easier to reconnect to others when we do not have to make them wrong.

Section 5: Short Essays on Conflict Resolution in Relationship

How to Move through Difficult Times

When two people reach an impasse in their relationship, neither person knows how to move forward. Both people feel overwhelmed, flooded with difficult feelings or cut off from any feelings. What can we do when we find ourselves in an impasse?

Unfortunately, the most common outcome of an impasse is ending the relationship. Separating seems to be one way of trying to handle the difficult and conflicting emotions we often feel trapped by. Being confronted with having to construct a separate life takes center stage and we leave this other set of uncomfortable feelings conveniently underground.

Seeking help through counseling or therapy can help. A therapist can help us recognize and express our own needs so that the relationship can begin to take care of us in a different way. We can identify unproductive patterns of relating or relational dynamics that have developed within our relationships. Being stuck in an unproductive dynamic can cause feelings and behaviors to repeat until we become conscious and recognize what is going on.

There are a few things we can do on our own. The first thing we can do is to look at our own feelings and behaviors to see if we can identify what roles we are playing out in our relationship. What ways are typical and repetitive? What feelings and behaviors have come up over and over again during the course of this relationship?

The second thing we can do is to sit with ourselves and figure out what emotional needs we are having that are not being met. We can focus on and imagine how we would like to be related to, asking ourselves what that would look and feel like. We can investigate our fears and ask why we are not expressing our feelings and needs. Are we afraid the other person does not care or does not want to hear our feelings? Are we uncomfortable with these needs? What do we know about ourselves that could help us understand this discomfort?

Here is an example of transforming a negative dynamic. Every time Mary did not call John when she was going to be late, or simply when he had not spoken to her for an extended period of time, he had the same set of negative emotions. He called these feelings "boredom." John was severely neglected as a child and when Mary did not call he associated to old feelings of abandonment and became frightened. He felt angry, neglected and disrespected.

John sat with himself and imagined what would relieve his boredom. He realized that calling Mary was what he wanted to do—to talk to her and to hear her voice. He felt uncomfortable realizing this need, and when she came home he was unable to say to her that he needed to hear her voice.

Usually in this situation, Mary would come home and find John withdrawn and angry. She had come to believe that she was the cause of his feelings, so she began to feel guilty and then got angry to avoid feeling the guilt. When Mary got angry, John withdrew even more. Their two sets of feelings formed a negative dynamic in their relationship.

One night, John interrupted this dynamic by telling Mary that he had figured out that when she did not call, he got upset. He let her know that he got upset because he needed to hear her voice.

Upon hearing him say that, Mary's defensive anger fell away. She was happy to respond to his needs when he expressed them directly, and they were both able to figure out a way of taking care of this need.

Talking about John's need relieved its intensity and together they figured out a way to work on his feelings of anxiety and boredom. By expressing the need, they both could work on a way of meeting the needs instead of getting stuck in their repetitive dynamic that frequently led them into an impasse.

Methods We Can Use to Resolve Conflicts

How to End Conflicts by Listening

Often, simply by deeply listening to another person, an ongoing conflict can be resolved. The skill of receiving the experience of another person, so that you actually are in attunement with them, can be the exact thing that is needed to end the disconnection created by a conflict.

This communication skill can be easily learned. In fact, we are biologically programmed to be good listeners. Why then is this essential element of communication so often unused, when it is so helpful in putting an end to our everyday conflicts?

Here are three fairly typical reasons why we find it hard to listen:

We are defending ourselves

Their feelings make us feel uncomfortable

Our need to be listened to is dominant

Defending ourselves

The first reason is that we are too busy defending ourselves to have room for another person's feelings or thoughts. When we are busy strategizing how we are right and how the other person isn't getting the picture, that is all that occupies our mental world.

In this case, we are not interested in what they are saying and what it means to them; we are interested only in making judgments about their feelings or thoughts. We are reacting to their thoughts and feelings only in relation to what we feel and think.

We find it difficult to hold and contain our own experience and keep it separate from the other person's, so that instead of reacting and defending, we can simply be present and be open to their experience.

Discomfort with another's feelings

Another common reason we find it hard to listen is that just being present and taking in what the other person is feeling can make us uncomfortable. We may think we are supposed to do something. We may feel it is not enough to just be there and listen.

Being present is something that we can all learn and value by practicing it in real-life situations. In this way, we soon realize that often the other person just needed to know that we can and want to receive what is going on with them, without having to do anything else. This simple act of listening implicitly says that we care.

Need to be heard overly active

And thirdly, when our minds are too busy defending, our inner narratives keep us from being able to hear the other person. It may be that our own need to be heard may be so active that we cannot quiet our minds enough to be present. It is important to recognize when this is happening.

It is possible in this situation to say to the other person that although you want to hear what they are saying, you are not able to be receptive. You can suggest that it might help if they listened to you first. It is often the case that in being heard, your need will be met and that you can have more room in your mind for the other.

Conflict Resolution: How to Stop Repetitive Arguments

Are you and your partner having the same reactions to the same situations over and over again? Does the other person's attitude or a behavior trigger a predictable and automatic response in you?

Have you reacted to a set of circumstances in the same way for as long as you can remember? Do you remember responding to your parents or a sibling in similar ways? Are you fed up with having the same negative reactions over and over again, but finding it difficult to make a change?

Obstacles to change

We all encounter obstacles to change. The first hurdle is the wanting that the other person should change. Rather than trying to change our response, we focus on what they are doing that is upsetting us.

Judging the other person as being at fault or being wrong makes us the good one, the right one. By finding fault in others we feel better about ourselves. We do so at the peril of getting locked into a position of blaming the other person.

Another obstacle to change is the belief that it is not possible to change because we are identified with our reactions. We have taken them to be an essential part of who we think we are.

We have become so accustomed to our reactions that they feel like an inseparable part of ourselves, like a leg or an arm. We believe that we are our reactions. They have given us a solid sense of being an individual self and we feel justified being that way. We end up not wanting to change.

It is liberating to realize that we can free ourselves from our habitual automatic reactions. There is a method for letting go of our automatic upsetting reactions. By letting go of old patterned responses and identifications, we can begin to see ourselves in new, more expansive ways. This takes patience and practice.

Keys to ending repetitive arguments:

- Wanting to change
- Realizing that change is up to us

- Understanding that our reactions are not caused by the other person
- Seeing the addictive quality of our reactions
- Examining what we gain by blaming the other person
- Learning what our triggers are
- Recognizing the feelings and needs these triggers bring up in us
- Developing an alternative method for meeting our needs

How to Be Present in Your Relationship

A big part of relating to another person is staying in the present with them and taking in immediate impressions of their actions, words and feelings and then being able to respond spontaneously. So often we are so desperately concerned with what impression we are making on others that we have little internal space for taking in any new impression of them.

As a result, we become limited in our perceptions of them. In this case, we limit our perceptions by how we are imagining them to be receiving us, and it may have nothing to do with what is actually going on with them. It is also hard to stay in the present moment with another person if we already have a well-formed preconception of who they are. Our preformed mental representation filters how we interpret any new impressions of them.

Our minds organize our experiences by bringing past associations to new experiences so that we quickly place new information into old categories and often miss the opportunity for a new experience. In order to prevent this automatic function from completely dominating how we take in new impressions, we have to make a conscious effort not to do so. If we cannot form new associations, we get stuck in repetitive experiences and often find ourselves stuck in the same old conflicts but with different people.

One reason we experience conflicts with others is that we habitually form a series of thoughts and feelings into a reaction. Our reactions become an emotional fact about our experience of someone else. We take our feelings to be facts. Often there is a judgment associated with this "fact," i.e., the other person has done something that has harmed us in some way and we feel angry or hurt and basically wronged.

We hold onto these "facts" in which there is already a narrative about what has happened and who said and did what and how we judge each of these actions. We make decisions as to how we want to relate to this person in the future based on these facts, often concluding that we do not want to relate to them. Sometimes our minds go over and over these narratives, adjusting them slightly here and there, as if rehearsing for a play. We position ourselves as if on a stage.

It is a difficult question to answer why we hold onto these emotional judgments. What do we gain by holding onto our "facts" when it seems that our emotional creations eliminate the room for new impressions, new interpretations, new information and new understandings of events or feelings about events? Our creations make it impossible to relate to the other person. We are now relating only to our own feelings about this person or event.

There are so many possible interpretations of our own behaviors, as often many things are going on within us at any one time, and there are equally as many possible causes for any other person's reactions. The intersection of any two people in an event that provokes either or both of them becomes a multilayered complexity that cannot be easily reduced to any one simple meaning.

When these complex emotional events are untangled by the process of each person telling their side of the experience and expressing their feelings, so that each person becomes aware of all the many layers of meaning, it becomes a challenge to hold onto a one-sided, simplistic position. Our emotional "facts" recede when we can hear the complexity of another person's experience and realize how little our "facts" have to do with what is going on for them.

Part of the process of untangling is to express what you really want the other person to hear about what has happened for you. By getting more in touch with your own need for having your experience recognized by the other person, and having that need met, you can relieve some of the need to cling to the narrative, your "fact." Sometimes our fixed narratives dissolve when they have been heard and understood by the other person.

Once either or both people in a conflict grasp the multilayered, often paradoxical nature of their own feelings and behaviors, their new perspective helps them to listen less defensively to the other person. They may come to see that the need to defend themselves by holding onto a preconceived position prevents them from being present and actually relating to the other person. Being less defensive is an opening to being more present.

Section 6: Short Essays on the Importance of Communication in Resolving Conflicts

Five Steps for Effective Communication in a Relationship

- Identify your thoughts, feelings and needs.

- Express yourself using "I" statements. Find your own voice.

- Ask for feedback to determine mutual understanding. Take responsibility for the delivery and reception of your message.

- Use non-defensive listening. Hear the other person's meaning— not yours. Listen for their intent. Take responsibility when you are not able to be present. If you are being defensive, express that.

- Reflect back. Be aware of how the other person hears things differently from you.

The first step in effective communication is to spend time alone to identify what you are feeling and thinking about the subject. Being present with yourself, allowing your thoughts and feelings to emerge, enables you to gain a fuller perspective on what you want to communicate. Asking yourself if there is something that you need from the other person that perhaps you have been unaware of can give you insight into some of the feelings you may be having.

The second step is to express these feelings and needs in direct, non-blaming ways to the other person. It is important to find your own voice, to say what your experience is and to express what you need in the relationship—even if you think they may not be able to get it. When you own what you are feeling and say in simple statements such as "I feel angry and I feel that you are not listening to what I am saying" or "I need you to take in my feelings and thoughts," you send a clear emotional message that takes responsibility for your own experience.

The third step is to introduce feedback into the communication by asking the other person to give you their reflection of your statement. You can inquire as to whether you were able to get your message across to them by suggesting that they now reflect back to you how they heard your message. If they reflect back accurately, you have achieved the first stage in mutual understanding. The next stage is for you to understand what they want to express. If they did not understand you, you can adjust how you are saying your message and ask them to try again to understand and reflect back what you are saying.

The fourth step involves effective listening. The first part of effective listening is to listen with an open, empathic mind so that the other person's message can reach you, and so that you can receive it without changing it with your own interpretation. It is very hard to simply hear what the other person is expressing without bringing our own filter to the task. The challenge is to recognize that every person has their own way of experiencing things—that each person's mental process evokes their own associations and meanings. We need to be open to the other person's ways of experiencing.

We can learn to be curious about how the other person's mind organizes what they experience followed by acceptance of their differences. Remembering differences, especially when you feel you are being criticized for something, is extremely hard. But even in that case, it is useful to try to understand how the other person is experiencing the situation. It is critical to remember that if another person's experience is different from ours, it does not make their experience right or wrong. It is just different. If we do not realize this, we tend to get defensive and caught in thinking about how right we are or how wrong the other person is.

When we cannot listen openly and are not able to put away our need to see things our way, it is important to express this, perhaps by saying, "I am not able to grasp what you are trying to express right now. My mind is caught up in other thoughts." Taking responsibility for not being able to be present and expressing that to the other person is a critical part of listening.

The fifth step is reflecting back what you have heard. After listening with an open and empathic mind, you will be able to simply say what you are hearing. The more accurately you can reflect back what the other person seems to be feeling, thinking or needing from you, the more the other person will feel recognized and understood. When both members of the relationship are able to provide an accurate reflection for the other person, mutual understanding is achieved. Mutual understanding is the cornerstone of effective communication.

How to Improve Communications

Most of us have learned how to communicate through a process of trial and error. We have developed our communication styles and skills primarily through the interactions we have had with our family and friends. Few of us have received formal communication training to develop our skills.

When we think of communication, ordinarily we think of it as a process in which someone speaks and someone listens. In normal communication, we wait politely for the other person to finish what they are saying so we can take our turn to talk. This model of communication places great value on speaking and little value on listening. Some of us may even have taken a speech class so that we could learn how to speak more effectively and be better understood.

Communication is the successful conveying and sharing of ideas and feelings. Each person who sends a message needs to know not only that his or her message was received, but that the other person understands what was meant. We all have a need to have our meaning understood. But because communication is context bound, this is often problematic. The listener may hear something entirely different from what was intended in the communication. A crude example of this is that if I say, "bark," you could think I was talking about the bark of a dog. But what I really was talking about was the bark of a tree. While this is a simple example, this level of misunderstanding often occurs in our communications.

An often missed element in communication is to find out how successful we are in sharing our thoughts and ideas. A simple way to do this is by inserting a feedback loop into our conversations to ensure that the listener has received the true intention of our communication. Adding a simple feedback loop can avoid misunderstanding and confusion. A feedback loop consists of the listener giving the speaker feedback about what he or she has heard them say. In all communications, we need at least two feedback loops because there are at least two people involved.

Because each person needs his or her meaning understood, we usually feel a disconnection when the other person mistakes what we have said. It can be confusing to say something and receive a response that seems to have nothing to do with what you meant. To further complicate matters, we may be confronted with all sorts of feelings and conclusions from the other person's reaction to what they thought we said. This can make the communication more difficult, as the person who has heard a different meaning and is reacting to it needs to be understood as well. Even though they did not understand your meaning, their meaning brings with it feelings that are now being communicated back to you for you to receive and understand.

How Incorporating Feedback Loops Helps Us Communicate Successfully

With awareness of the feedback model, you may as a speaker ask the other person to say back to you what you just said. If you ask the other person for their feedback in the interest of ensuring that you have spoken clearly, you will have an opportunity to correct anything that was inaccurately heard or misinterpreted.

If the person listening has already reacted strongly to what you have said, a second feedback loop can be introduced. You can say, "I think you may have misunderstood what I said, but now I want to see if I can understand what your reaction is about." Once you have given them feedback, shown them that you understand their reaction, and that you are following what they are saying or feeling, the possibility of your original message being received and understood increases.

You can then return to the original message and introduce the first feedback loop. If the other person has realized that their reaction was to some meaning other than what you had originally intended, they will now more likely be able to understand your original meaning. With the use of the double feedback model it is much more possible to achieve mutual understanding.

Section 7: Understanding and Using TruceWorks.com or the Mobile App

Introduction

The TruceWorks website takes advantage of the Internet's ability to facilitate communication. It is both an educational resource providing written information for gaining new perspectives on relationships and an introduction to its users to a written experiential process known as the CLEAR process. The CLEAR process creates a forum for the simultaneous intersection of two people's written points of view, which are displayed side by side on the screen. The process gives each member a perspective from which to digest and express their own experience and have quick reference to the digested experience of the other person. A written process gives the time and space to think and respond instead of speaking only in reaction to what someone else has triggered in us. By each person using a step-by-step format, both participants are supported to express and listen—two essentials of building connection.

The TruceWorks CLEAR Process

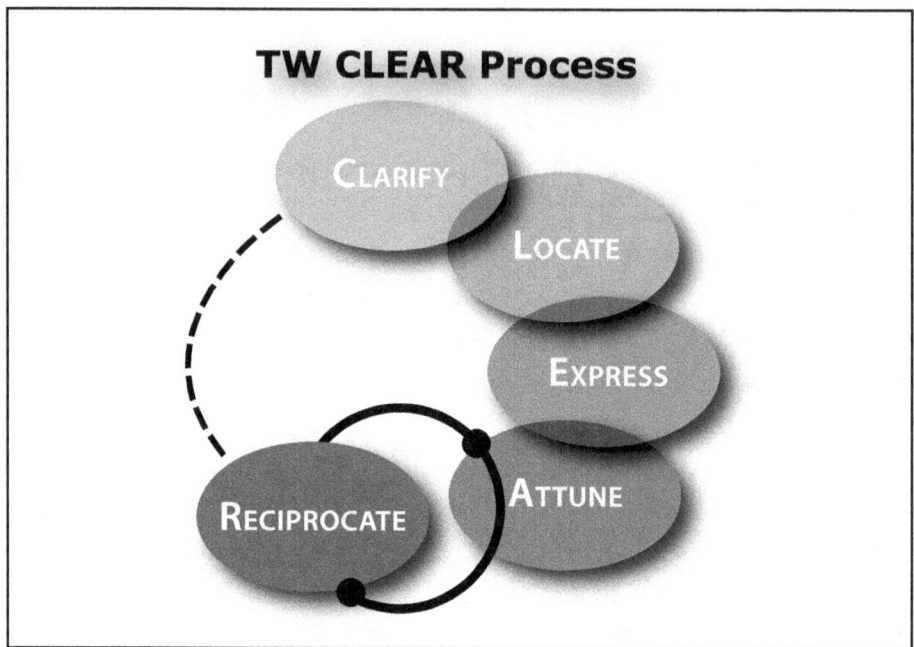

Origins and Purpose of the CLEAR Relational Process

The TruceWorks CLEAR process combines relation-based communication theory with principles of non-violent communication. It is designed to support two members in a guided exchange of messages and responses to resolve everyday conflicts.

Non-violent principles give guidance to people to express their feelings in a nonjudgmental way and suggest that under our most reactive emotions are relational needs that are not being met. Being able to focus on our needs and to express them in language that encourages communication is essential to the ending of conflicts.

Learning to express our needs in relationship to others, so that we are responded to by having our needs recognized and hopefully met, and learning to reciprocate, whereby we also learn to respond to other people's needs, is fundamental to human growth as well as to resolution of conflicts.

Because our basic needs are met in relationship, when our relationships are disrupted, as they are in conflicts, we need to be able to reestablish our connection with others. The CLEAR process structures our communication so that we are receiving and giving more attuned and reciprocal responses and this helps establish reconnection.

The five questions and two response boxes of the CLEAR communication process recreate basic relational dynamics that provide an experience of being responded to and responding to another person in ways that can actually meet some of our relational needs. Conflicts result when basic relational needs are not being met.

How the CLEAR Process Promotes Connection

Most people have never learned the relational skills that would help them learn to stop reacting to the familiar triggers that are set off by their partner's words or actions, nor have they learned to communicate in a way that could bring a sense of connection into the relationship when disconnection occurs.

Optimal communication promotes a strengthening of the understanding between two people. It is important that each person is invited to express their thoughts and feelings and that the messages sent are received by the other person in a way in which the sender feels heard and understood. With feedback this is more easily achieved.

The CLEAR Process Is Designed to Facilitate a Two-Way Feedback Dynamic in a Conversation

It is often difficult in a relationship to remember that there are two sets of messages that need to be received, one set from each person. When one person sends out a signal, they are expecting that this message will be taken in and responded to in a way that indicates that this has occurred. If, instead of getting a response that indicates their message has been received, the second person has simply used the first person's message as an opportunity to express their own message, the first person cannot feel heard—and a miscommunication has occurred. Both people have to remember that they need to send out messages and that they also need to respond to the other person's messages. This dynamic needs to be a mutual one.

The CLEAR Process Is Designed to Mimic the Early Relational Dynamic between a Parent and Child

Because of the positive developmental impact on a baby when their signals are responded to contingently, that is, when the parent makes an effort to comprehend what is going on in their child's experience instead of imposing onto the child their own sense of what is going on, we have attempted to provide this form of exchange in the CLEAR process. When two people are willing to take in what the other person is feeling without imposing their own reaction onto them, one person feels heard and contained by the other, giving them more psychological space to reciprocate, i.e., hear and contain the other person.

How to Use the CLEAR Process on the Website or on the TruceWorks App

The TruceWorks website and app support the operation of the CLEAR process—an interactive communication process that can be used between any two people in the world. The users fill out the five questions and response forms, which structures the communication they send to the other person. Both persons' responses can be viewed simultaneously on the screen, and by following the sequenced question and response forms, a more relational communication experience can occur.

Both the website and the app provide help instructions throughout the process and generic examples of conflicts resolved by this process to review.

The Stages of the CLEAR Process Require Answering the Five-Step Questions and the Two-Step Response Form

Question #1: What happened?

To answer the first question, you are guided to clarify your response. In most cases, the trigger to our emotional reaction is some behavior, attitude or statement by the other person. When you have strong feelings, you may find it hard to articulate them. You may find that the best you can do is to get angry, hurt or withdraw.

Formulating for yourself your own narrative as to what has happened is important, although we typically see what has happened as a result of what the other person has done "to us" and feel that they have caused our feelings. We may blame the other person for our feelings. We may get mad at them or feel hurt by them. Being able to narrate what happened—the event that triggered you—is the first step.

The first stage of the CLEAR process is called Clarify. Here you are asked to express what happened without blaming. You write down the facts of the event as you see them without accusing the other person of doing anything. You are being asked to say only "What happened to you"?

During this stage, it is important to be aware that we often see the other person through our own lens. It is a huge step in our personal growth when we realize that how we experience another person's behavior or words is often not how they were intended and that the other person's understanding of the same event may be quite different from ours. Staying open to this possibility and simply stating what happened for you helps you clarify your experience and separate it from how the other person is viewing it.

Question #2: How did it make you feel?

The second stage is to locate your feelings. Having an emotional reaction, getting angry, sad or fearful, is not the same as telling someone how you feel. Feelings are complicated emotional events having long and very personal histories. Learn to locate your feelings by stopping and asking yourself the question, what am I feeling? When the other person said or did XYZ, what did I feel?

Question #3: What are your needs in this situation?

In this question you are asked to locate your needs. Asking yourself what need was unmet that gave rise to the feelings is the next stage in this process. Asking and answering these questions for yourself is a skill you will learn with practice and focus. Our needs that we have in relationships often go unnoticed. Learning to identify these needs and **expressing** them brings clarity to our reactions both for us and for the other person. (A list of relational needs and an explanation of them is available by using the help instructions found on each question and response.)

After you have located your feelings and needs to your best ability, it is important to put them into words. You may find that when you express how you feel, the emotional charge diminishes and it becomes easier to communicate. It is a true act of responsibility to own and communicate your feelings.

Once you have translated the emotional energy into thought, and then put those thoughts into words, you can express yourself. It is often possible for the other person to identify with what you are saying and to receive and accept why you are feeling angry or hurt.

By expressing yourself, you are transforming your emotional energy into meaningful bits of information so that the other person can take it in and with you share your meaning.

Question #4: What do you want the other person to understand?

Answering the question, "What do you want understood?" is another aspect of **expressing** yourself. Formulating the answer to this question will focus you on what you want the other person to take in about your experience. It puts you into a more relational position and encourages you to distinguish what is specifically important to you for the other person to understand. It is a direct expression of your relational needs, in that it is asking the other person to take in a part of your experience.

Question # 5: What do you request from the other person?

This question focuses you on what you need and what you want to ask from the other person. **Expressing** your needs directly and clearly does not mean that you will get all of them met. It gives you a stronger sense of yourself and from there you can more easily negotiate without feeling compromised.

Response #1: Reflect back what the other person has asked you to understand

The fourth stage in the CLEAR process is **Attunement.** In reflecting back on our response form, we are attuning to the other person's statement of the thoughts and feelings that they want us to understand. We will also be receiving their feedback on how accurately we were able to do this.

Both you and the person with whom you are in conflict need attunement. You need to both receive it and give it. If you have a feeling or a need that another person is not getting, you may experience an increased need for them to understand and to give you the evidence that they actually do. When the other person understands and they reflect back to you that they really have taken in what you are feeling or needing, you feel their attunement.

It is important to be able to attune to the other person as well. You can do this by empathizing, taking in and being curious about how they are experiencing things and then reflecting back to them what they want us to understand. Mutual attunement reconnects you with the other person and gives you the foundation for the next step.

Response #2: Please respond to the requests made by the other person

The fifth stage is **Reciprocation.** In all relationships there is give and take. Your willingness to negotiate is critical. Ask for what you need. Stay open to the other's responses as well as their requests of you. Asking for something does not always mean receiving exactly what you have requested. The act of reciprocation will often end the present conflict. It is important to differentiate between your bottom line and those things that you feel okay about compromising on.

From Disconnection to Connection

How the Five Stages of the CLEAR Process Build Connection

These are the five stages of the CLEAR communication process which facilitate reconnection with another person that you are in conflict with.

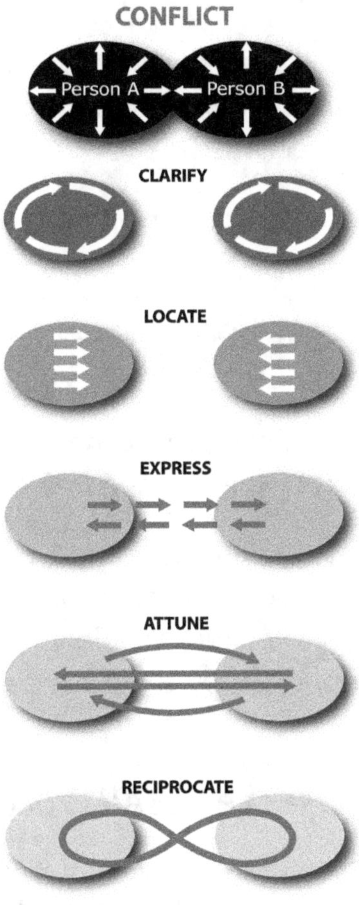

CONFLICT

Person A — Person B

CLARIFY
See Question 1.
Distinguishing feelings about conflict from what happened.

CLARIFY

LOCATE
See Questions 2 & 3
Identifying feelings and needs.

LOCATE

EXPRESS
See Question 4
Saying what you want the other person to understand.

EXPRESS

ATTUNE
See Reflect Box
Reflect back your understanding.

ATTUNE

RECIPROCATE
See Question 5 &
Response Box
Asking for what you need and offering what you can give.

RECIPROCATE

The Five Stages of the CLEAR Process Diagram

The CLEAR (an acronym) process has five stages. It is based on a relational model that mimics the preverbal communication patterns that promote psychological development.

This diagram represents the communication process that directs the reconnection.

The two circles represent conflict between two people. Part of each circle is merged with the other.

In the first stage, each circle represents two people clarifying what happened for them.

In the second stage, they locate their feelings and needs, as shown by the two circles representing each person organizing their own thoughts and feelings.

In the third stage, each person expresses to the other their thoughts and feelings.

In the fourth stage, each circle represents the giving and receiving of feedback, creating more connection between them.

In the fifth and final stage, connection has been restored between the two circles by the give and take of negotiation.

These five stages are generated by and correspond to the five questions each person answers and the responses they give. These stages serve to redirect the flow of communication so that each person is supported by the other person's responses to feel more connection.

Who Can Use the CLEAR Process?

Any two people, anywhere, who want to use a written process to either repair or deepen their connection with each other.

How to Use the CLEAR Process on Your Computer

There are two ways to use the TruceWorks CLEAR process: asynchronously (not at the same time) with anyone in the world, each person using their own computer, or synchronously (at the same time), where you can do the process with someone on the same computer at the same time.

After you log in, you will be taken to a personalized dashboard where you can start new conversations or access existing ones.

Asynchronous process

You will fill out and submit a five-step CLEAR form. Help prompts are included throughout the process.

By submitting the five-step form, an email invitation will be sent to your friend, colleague or family member, inviting them to use the TruceWorks website. If they choose to participate, they will be able to read and respond to your statements by filling out and submitting their own five-step CLEAR form and/or the two-step response form.

By selecting the current conversation on your dashboard, you will each be able to view the full conversation (both persons' responses posted side by side). After you have read each other's responses, continue to use the two-step response form as many times as you need to achieve mutual understanding and resolution.

When you select and click on the Resolved box for this conversation, an email will be sent to notify the other person that you feel the conflict has been resolved. The process continues until both of you feel resolved. You can select to archive both resolved and unresolved conversations for future reference or delete them from your dashboard.

Synchronous process

You may choose to work on resolving your conflict with a friend, colleague or family member by using the CLEAR process together on the same computer. Click on the Start button, follow the prompts and simply hand the computer back and forth to make your entries. Either person can begin.

Enter the name of the person you are resolving a conflict with.

The first person fills out and submits a five-step CLEAR form. Help prompts are included throughout the process.

The second person views the display of the first person's statements and responds by filling out their own five-step form and/or by using the two-step response form.

The first person views this conversation displayed side by side and responds using the two-step form. Conversation continues using the two-step form until both parties let the other person know they feel resolved.

Conversations may be archived for future reference or deleted.

It may be useful to repeat the process for unresolved conversations.

The TruceWorks Mobile App

The TruceWorks mobile app is a conjunct of TruceWorks.com. After downloading the app the user is taken back to the web site to sign up and/or to accept or decline a new conversation invitation from another user. Other than these preliminary actions, the user of the TruceWorks app can follow all their conversation threads on their mobile, respond or initiate a new conversation. An email is sent to notify each user of another user's response. A link on the email takes you back to the website or you can open your app, log in, refresh (slide the screen down) and find all of your conversations posted sequentially. *The TruceWorks mobile app is in development and will be launched in Winter 2011.*

SECTION 8: TruceWorks.com: Navigating the Website

How do you get around on the website?

The Homepage and what happens when you log in.

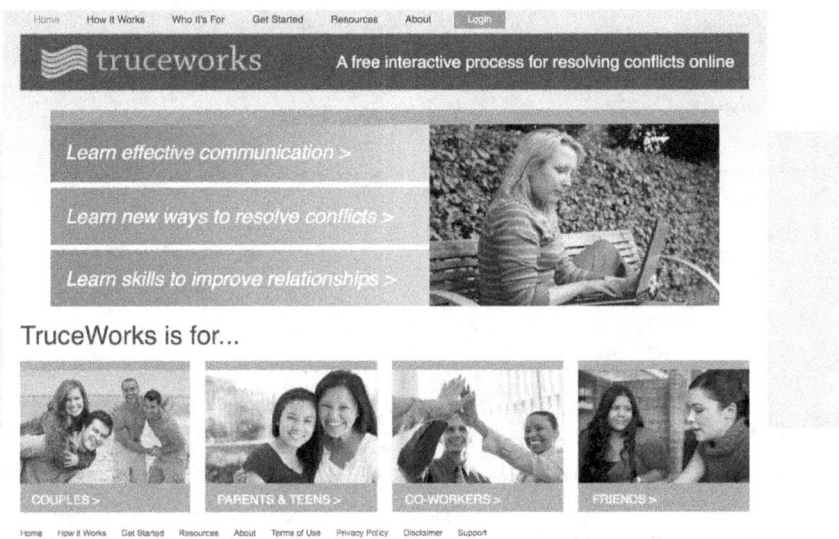

Welcome to TruceWorks. You may want to look around the website. Visit the Resource Library or you can go to a section of the site written for couples, parents and teens, friends, or co-workers by clicking on one of the "TruceWorks is for" windows.

You will go to a page such as the one you see here. You can read to see if you want to try out the process, in which case you can begin by clicking on Start.

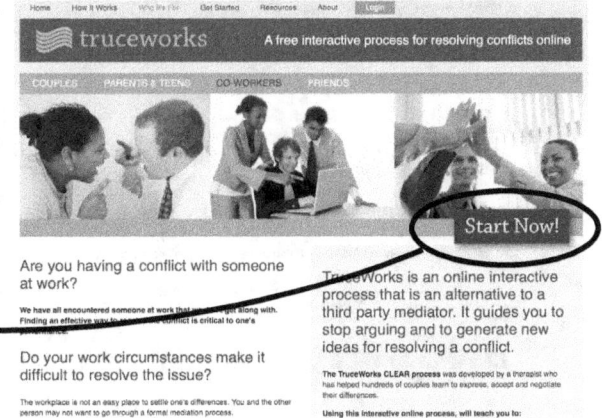

Here is the sign-up/log-in page.

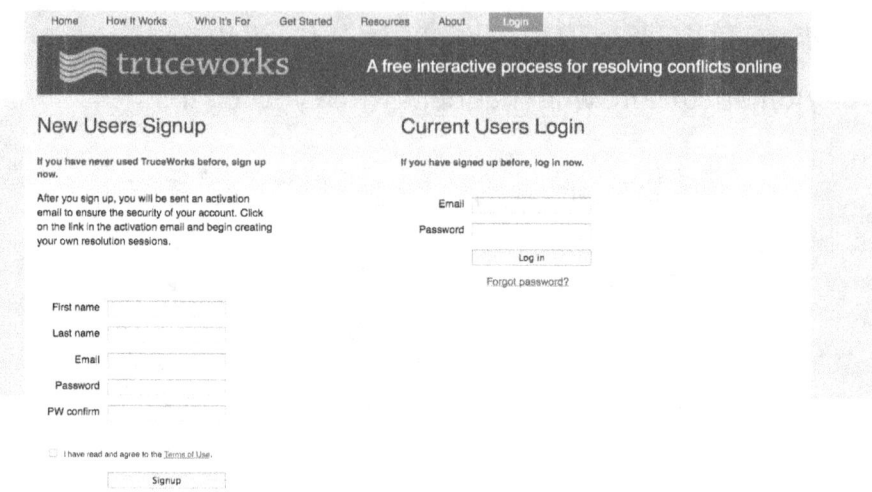

The site asks you to agree to the terms of service. You can always unsubscribe if you find you do not want to use TruceWorks.com.

After you log in, you will go to your dashboard (second screen below) where all the conversations you have will be logged. For now, you click on Start a New Conversation and fill out and send the five-step form.

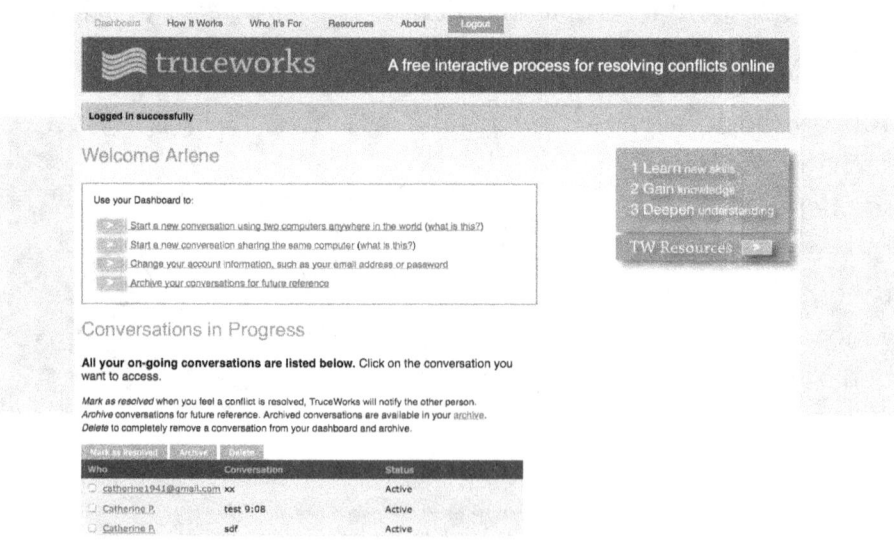

Below, you will see the five-step questions and the response form. After filling these out, the site will send an email to your partner inviting them to participate.

Five-step CLEAR Process Form

The following online process is designed to help you learn to communicate and resolve conflicts with one another. *Fill out all the steps and use the instructions.* Using the help tips in the instruction links, opens up an opportunity to learn a new way to communicate.

1. What Happened?

2. How did it make you feel?

3. What are your needs in this situation?

4. What do you want the other person to understand?

5. What do you request from the other person?

CLEAR Response Form

1. Please reflect back what the other person has asked you to understand.

2. Use this box for any response you want to make to the other person.

While filling out these questions, the site provides you with the information and guidance you may need to have a useful dialogue with your partner.

Following these instructions will hopefully produce a conversation where both you and your partner feel you have expressed yourself clearly, have had time to consider what you want to say, and have been open to reading and responding to what they have said.

The screen shot below shows you what it will look like. Helen R. has filled out her five-step form and she has sent the invitation to Julie R. Below, you can see that both conversations are posted alongside each other and that further responses will be shown as they are posted, one after the other. You can respond as many times as you want and are guided to respond to what the other person has said so that they can see that you are taking in what they are feeling.

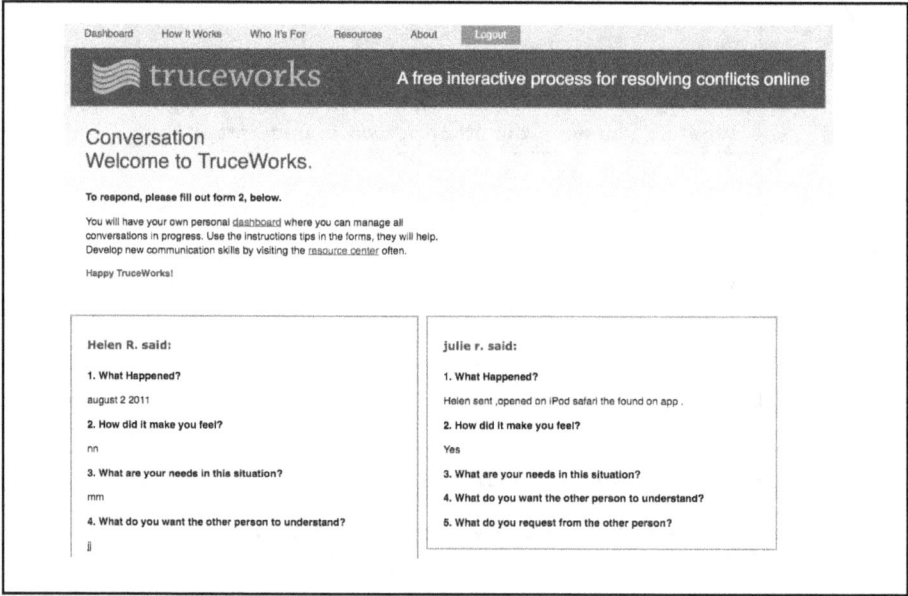

Once both people have used the response boxes to give feedback to the other person and negotiate with them what you need to end the conflict, you return to your dashboard and click the Resolved button. Your partner will be notified that your conflict with them is resolved, and if they need more response from you, the conversation will remain active until you receive a notification of their resolution. You can save or delete your conversations.

The Resource Library is available to you at any time to read more about relationships, communication and conflict resolution.

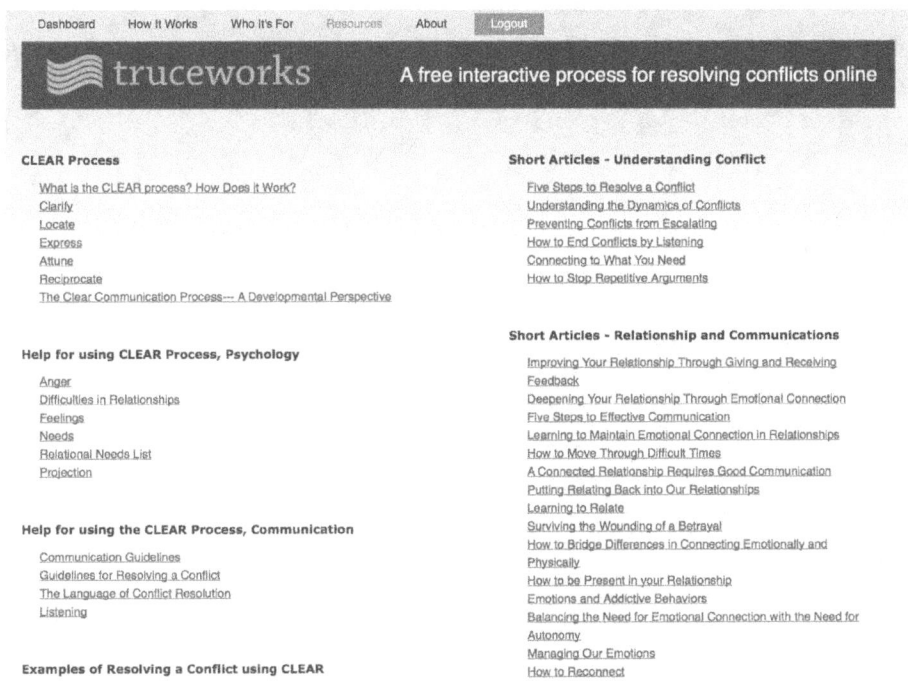

ABOUT THE AUTHOR

Julie Roberts lives and works in San Francisco, Petaluma and East Calais, Vermont.

She is a mom, a grandma, and a therapist. She practices yoga and meditation.

www.ingramcontent.com/pod-product-compliance
Lightning Source LLC
Chambersburg PA
CBHW070201290526
45789CB00002B/862